The schools work
HANDBOOK

The schools work HANDBOOK

Serving God in your local school

Emlyn Williams

SCRIPTURE UNION

Scripture Union, 207–209 Queensway, Bletchley, Milton Keynes, MK2 2EB, England.

First published 1996

ISBN 0 86201 951 6

British Library Cataloguing-in-Publication Data
A catalogue record for this book is available from the British Library.

Cover illustration by Chris Masters.
Cover design by Mark Carpenter Design Consultants.

Phototypeset by Intype London Ltd.
Printed and bound in Great Britain by Cox & Wyman Ltd, Reading.

To Anna and Tom

CONTENTS

PREFACE

Unlike most people, I never really left school. Over the years I have been a pupil, a teacher, a schools worker and a parent. It all began when I entered the nursery class at the age of three, and, frankly, I never thought that my education would take so long!

However, if school has been an important strand running through my life, God has been an even more significant one. Not surprisingly, over the years I have come to realise how the two strands were entwined. This book, therefore, is an attempt to say something about how Christians can share in God's concern for schools and, more importantly, the people in them.

Much has been written about education, evangelism, children's work, youth work and the like, but as far as I know there is very little on the kinds of things covered in this book. There is much more to be said, and I am aware of this book's weaknesses and limitations. Nevertheless, I pray that the results of its writing will be more and more Christians, both inside and outside school communities, discovering how they can serve God in schools. Since the next generation is in school right now, what could be a higher calling?

What I have written I have learnt from the many people I have come to know through my involvement with schools, and I am grateful to them all. My colleagues in Scripture Union, especially in England and Australia, have endured a great deal at my hands (!) but have also given a great deal.

And 'Tricia, my wife, (whom I first met as a fellow Scripture Union schools worker) has not only supported me in all of this but also paved the way with an earlier book on similar themes (*Christians in school?*, Scripture Union). To all these people I offer my inadequate but sincere thanks.

WHY WORK IN SCHOOLS?

Schools are big business. There are more than 27,000 schools in England alone. We spend about £19 billion on them each year. Every day we entrust over 8 million of our children to the care of 500,000 teachers along with the many more administrators, cleaners and technicians so essential to schools today.

Over the past few years Christians have shown an increasing interest in schools. As schools have developed closer links with the community, so individuals have found ways of becoming involved at a local level. More and more churches have developed relationships with the schools in their area, and some have even appointed paid staff to this ministry. This book aims to help such people think through their work, and to equip them so that they are more effective.

However, this book is also for another group of people – those who think that working with the young is not for them. I believe that schools and youth work should be the concern of the whole church – not just those with a particular calling to it – as the whole church is called to mission. Obviously, we cannot all be involved in everything, but we need to be aware of the current educational trends and the possibilities for sharing the Christian message, to know what God is doing and where he is working. If you are a reluctant schools worker, I hope that this book will do more than just help you to become better informed. Schools work is not just for children's and youth workers. As schools and communities work together more closely, so the opportunities increase for all kinds of people to consider what they might do.

It is less common in the 1990s to hear the young spoken of as 'the church of tomorrow' – most of us have woken up to the fact that they are part of the church of today. It is still common, however, to find the attitude that *real* mission is to adults. Don't get me wrong. I am not saying we should all drop everything and get involved in schools work, and I am certainly not saying that it is a panacea, the answer to all our problems. However, if we are serious about mission to the world, we cannot afford to ignore ministry to schools: it raises important issues for us all.

Every book comes from a context, and this is no exception. Most of my experience has been in state schools in England. Nevertheless, I have also tried to draw from my experience of working in Australia, and I have taken into account the differing situations in other parts of the United Kingdom. Having said this, you should find that much of what this book says is relevant to schools in general, whatever brand and wherever they are. I trust that it will help you to play your part in the 'mission field in our own backyard'.

1

MISSION DOWN THE STREET

It's 3.14 pm, and a quiet street near our home has just undergone its twice-daily transition into a traffic jam. Cars of all ages and makes block the street while adults and children weave their way through the congestion on foot or on bikes. Cars, bikes, baby buggies and their drivers have all converged on a small primary school to make sure that the next generation gets home safely in time to watch Children's TV and *Neighbours*. One minute from now the crowd will more than double as the school discharges into the waiting world the 200 reasons for its existence.

At first glance the crowd consists of just the kind of people you would expect outside a school. There are lots of mums, quite a few dads, a number of pre-schoolers waiting for the day when they too will be collected. Some of the adults have lived in the town all their lives; for others this is one more stop on a tour that has taken them around the country and beyond. Many were at work this morning, and others will be going this evening; but for some work is only a dream. Just about every kind of parent the dictionary can think of is somewhere here: single parents, step-parents, foster parents, grandparents, and many who are just parents, plain and simple.

This slice of life is about as varied as you will find any-where. In a world of increasing diversity few other places, apart from the supermarket, bring such a wide range of people into regular contact with each other. No wonder some have likened the school gate to the biblical well – it is a crucial hub of the community. And this is why ministry to schools is a vital part of the mission of the church.

SCHOOLS MATTER

> I strongly suspect that if Paul were here today, he would elect to be an ISCF staff worker, or at least he'd assign Timothy or one of Philip's daughters to be one!
>
> Brian V Hill, 'The potential of our schools work', *Catalyst 4*,
> Scripture Union International, p 24

> [For 'ISCF staff worker' read 'schools worker'.]

These are the words of Brian Hill, Professor of Education at Murdoch University in Perth, Western Australia. (At one stage in his career he was a schools worker with Scripture Union, probably unique amongst professors of education!) His point is simply that the kind of strategic thinking that led Paul to spread the gospel as he did in the first century would today lead him into schools work. It is not just sentimental attachment to his own past that makes Hill argue so strongly for schools work. It is his recognition of the significant place schools have in society. All of us – not just parents and children – are affected by the work that schools do. This is why countries everywhere are prepared to spend such a large proportion of their national income on educating the young.

What is it that makes schools so important? Why are we all concerned about them? We might find some answers by looking at two crucial aspects of schools.

WHAT SCHOOLS DO

Schools shape the future

The workers, parents, thinkers, politicians, entrepreneurs, artists and criminals of the next generation are being educated right now. For six to seven hours a day, over a period of at least eleven years, they are under the influence of school. What goes on during those hours will have a major impact on the kind of adults they become. Not everything will have the desired effect. Sometimes the influence of school will be counter-productive. But be sure of one thing: after 15,000 hours of school those people will not be the same as they were before.

What we do with and to our schools therefore reflects what we want for the future. The introduction of non-selective schools in Britain in the 1960s and 1970s was an attempt to improve the efficiency of educational organisation. What this said, in effect, was that we wanted a society where people had equal opportunity. We did not want the opportunities available to people to be restricted by decisions made about them when they were eleven. Consider the current curriculum emphasis in many parts of the world on maths, science and technology. It is a statement that these countries want to be nations with a technically skilled workforce, to meet the perceived needs of industry. Of course we can argue about the respective merits of these and other policies, but the fact remains that the decisions we make about education are informed by our dreams for the future.

Christians have a great tradition of concern for the future of society. The biblical principle of 'loving your neighbour' stands against the individualism that is unconcerned about others. Wilberforce and his relentless campaign against slavery, Shaftesbury and his concern about child labour, and Mother Theresa and her work with the dying in Calcutta are the often quoted examples, yet they are only the luminaries in a host of other less well known Christians who are actively 'loving their neighbours'. The logical extension of this commitment is concern for the future that education and schools are bringing about.

Schools pass on values
Schools are not neutral. They are built on a whole raft of values, some more controversial than others. A school

15

cannot separate an area of a person called 'mind' and develop that, leaving the rest of the person unchanged.

Our society recognises this and therefore has high expectations of schools and their ability to communicate positive values. There are regular calls for them to 'teach the difference between right and wrong'. When a moral problem is recognised, there is the inevitable cry 'What on earth are the schools doing?' In one recent celebrated case of juvenile criminal behaviour, the judge criticised the boy's school yet never mentioned the responsibility of his mother and father. We have such high expectations of schools' ability to transmit values that, if necessary, we will expect them to override what we see as defective or delinquent parenting.

However, it is not only through explicit moral teaching that schools transmit values. The ethos of a school is very powerful in this respect and, of course, schools differ greatly. Some emphasise individual achievement, other co-operation and teamwork. Success may be much valued, or recognition given to straightforward effort. Some schools communicate moral absolutes, others present morality as relative.

The values of a school may be made quite explicit. I taught in a state school where every pupil wore a blazer badge with the school motto 'With God to the summits'! But even where values are not stated quite so obviously they may, nevertheless, be very clear to those involved. A friend of mine says that the only people who were ever publicly recognised in her old school were those who achieved academic or sporting success. What does that say to the not-very-academic musician, to take just one example? Conversely, I heard Sir John Harvey-Jones, the businessman, speaking about an independent school of which he was a governor. He said that each term every pupil received public recognition of something they had achieved. The challenge was for the school to identify that achievement no matter how small it might be.

So far we have looked only at the formal impact of

schools on values. However, school is about much more than what its administration organises and plans. School is about being with other young people, and their impact may be greater than anything over which the school has control. Taking children out of their homes and placing them in a wider community inevitably influences the values they hold. When the five-year-old uses a choice expletive and tells you that she learnt it at school, she is probably not talking about what took place in an English lesson!

If we are serious about influencing the values of the next generation, we must be serious about schools. Certainly the home and the media play their part, but the experience of school is still one of the major influences on the values of our young people and we cannot afford *not* to be involved.

Schools offer opportunity

Around the world, education is seen as a step onto the ladder of opportunity. Westerners who have taught in developing countries speak of the eagerness of pupils to learn, particularly in comparison with many of their counterparts here. Families make great sacrifices in order for their children to be educated. And the reason? They see education as a sure way to prosperity and the possibility of a better life.

This is not just wishful thinking on the part of ambitious families. Governments also recognise the opportunities brought by education. Many so-called 'first-world' countries have given large amounts in foreign aid to developing countries for them to improve their education systems. The belief is that this will equip their populations to bring about economic development and thus new opportunity to the nation as a whole. Around the world, education is transforming people's lives by opening them up to all kinds of new possibilities.

From a Christian point of view we rejoice when people are given the opportunity of a different and better future.

However, a better future is not just about a better job or more money or greater power. The gospel is at the heart of the better future that God offers and if that possibility is not presented the future offered is deficient.

WHAT SCHOOLS ARE

Schools are for everyone
One of the great civilising influences in the world has been universal education. The principle that education should be available to everyone, and not just the rich, has transformed many countries in our world. We may well have reservations about just how much schooling can achieve, but there is no doubt that it has brought great benefit. Its impact has been social as well as educational. Because everyone goes to school, schools have become the great 'melting pots' of our communities.

This is very significant for mission, because the whole thrust of the gospel is that God's concern is for the whole world. Therefore, Christians can never be content to be part of a low-profile, minority interest group. We are called to be right in the midst of the melting pot.

Increasingly, however, we are sidelined when it comes to contact with young people. In 1955, the year before I started school, 83% of the population of Britain had had significant contact with the church when they were young, through Sunday School, youth groups and the like. Only 6% had no contact at all. By 1989 the picture was the complete reverse. At best, less than 14% of young people had any significant contact with the church and more than 85% had no links at all (*All God's Children?*, National Society, pp 3, 4). This sea change has happened in my lifetime. (To the best of my knowledge there is no connection between the two!) So, what do we do about it? How do we make contact with the vast majority for whom the Christian church is as far outside their experience as interplanetary travel?!

Paul faced this issue when he was in the process of

establishing the early Christians in churches. How could he make contact with people? He had no building into which he could invite them, so he did the obvious thing and went to where they were; and this was usually somewhere like the market-place. Schools may be described as the modern-day equivalents of the market-place. In Britain at least, almost everyone attends school, regardless of their social class or background. Therefore, if we are serious about influencing a whole generation, schools are an obvious starting place though by no means the only significant arena.

Schools are communities
When I was a teacher, there was one day each year when everything ran perfectly smoothly. It was the day before term started. The staff were all there but no pupils came along to mess up our plans. Smooth though that day was, however, it was actually quite unreal. Because schools are not simply organisations: they are communities, and communities are where we have to share the gospel.

In the New Testament the gospel is usually brought to people in the context of relationships. Paul reminded the Thessalonians that he and the other apostles had shared 'not only the gospel of God but our lives as well' (1 Thess 2:8). This is a great principle, because when the gospel is brought in this way it is seen as well as heard. It is demonstrated in the power of the Spirit.

Even more significant is the fact that God himself brought the good news to us just like this: 'The Word became flesh and dwelt among us' (John 1:14). The Incarnation is a crucial pattern for us in our ministry. Lives and words go together.

We have established that schools are important for mission because of their nature as communities. And, as communities, they may well have the advantage of including Christian pupils or teachers in their number. So often I hear people talk about 'trying to get into' a school as though any

Christian ministry in it is impossible until a speaker or evangelist can visit. Yet the fact is that there are almost certainly Christians in the school already, who would be even more effective in their witness if they were only encouraged or mobilised. One of our priorities in ministry to schools has to be to help Christians *in situ* in this way.

Schools are at the heart of the larger community

Think back to the beginning of this chapter, to that group outside my children's school. It is a hub of the local community. It is made up of representatives of perhaps 150 families who meet at least twice a day for most of the year, more regularly than any church I know. The group has a joint purpose in the education of its children. The people in that group may have almost nothing else in common other than the fact that their children go to the same school, yet in this they are brought together into regular relationship with and commitment to each other. The school's influence is wider still – the local community as a whole has an interest in what it achieves. You can be sure that if something goes wrong in the school the local council and press will be very interested. In other words, a school and the people who make up its community form one of the basic building blocks of local society. No wonder we need to take schools seriously if we are concerned about mission.

Just as the gospel can be shared relationally with the school, it can spread in the same way through the wider school community and through the local community as a whole. Indeed, there are local churches that have come into being because young people in school have become Christians, and the gospel has spread to their families and beyond.

Schools are market-places of ideas

Schools work hard at getting their pupils to think, at introducing them to ideas. In a society as diverse as ours almost everything is on offer. If we believe therefore that the Christian message is true and important, it is vital that we go into this supermarket of ideas. If we don't, we will have no excuse if the 'product unavailable' sticker appears on the shelf where Christianity should be.

Many Christians feel uncomfortable with the Christian faith sitting alongside a whole range of religions, philosophies and ideas. We have been used to operating in a society which is at least nominally Christian and which has given Christianity special privileges. Yet the first Christians didn't experience any privileges and the world doesn't offer us any now. If we are going to get anywhere at all with mission, we have to come to terms with being stacked on the shelf alongside everything else. It may be uncomfortable. We may even face unfair prejudice, often in reaction to our previous dominance. But we cannot afford to ignore the 'supermarkets' and only operate from our own stores! As Australian bishop Bruce Wilson wrote, withdrawing from state schools is, for the church, 'the equivalent of digging your own grave before you suicide' (Bruce Wilson, *Can God survive in Australia?*, Albatross, p 154).

Ideas can sound theoretical and impersonal but in fact they affect real people's lives. Recognising this can be a powerful motivation to do something. I met a lady in St Petersburg, Russia, who told me why she had voluntarily started to teach religious education in a school. She had overheard some of her son's friends talking about reincarnation and realised that, although they knew about all kinds of similar ideas, unless someone told them they would never know about Jesus. This was all the motivation she needed to get on and do something.

The future, values, opportunity, community, ideas – all of these are vital themes for Christians. In schools we meet them head-on. This is why we cannot afford to leave schools work on the sidelines if we are serious about mission. The great thing is that in Britain at least we are not starting from scratch. There is a long tradition of Christian involvement in schools. The first schools were started by the churches, many later becoming a major part of the state system. Even today one in four schools is a denominational school, catering for a much wider section of the population than just the regular church community.

However, Christian involvement goes much further than the existence of church schools. As mentioned above, significant numbers of Christians are professionally involved in schools, as teachers, administrators and workers of all kinds. And, of course, as pupils. Whilst school is often a difficult arena for many of them, they can have a remarkable impact there for the gospel. The existence of religious education and collective worship means that there is explicit discussion and presentation of religious issues, often with the assistance of Christians from the local community. Undergirding this is the everyday involvement of Christians acting as salt and light, supporting the work of schools as parents, helpers and governors. Making the most of these opportunities is what the rest of this book is about.

2

JUST WHAT'S GOING ON IN SCHOOLS?

- It is 1.30 pm on Friday. A class of primary school children has just settled into the afternoon routine. A welcome peace replaces the noise and excitement of the lunch break. In an empty classroom, four mums of children in the school are chatting and drinking coffee. Around them three of their toddlers are having a great time playing with some toys. This is one of the two occasions each term when these parents meet to pray for the school. They started meeting a couple of years ago in one of their homes but, when the school heard about this, the head teacher suggested that they might sometimes like to meet in school.

- Simon is a sixth-former studying English. In the last lesson they discussed a novel with a very bleak outlook on life. Afterwards, a group of students continued chatting over coffee. They ended up talking about life, the universe and everything. Simon didn't say much, but eventually one of his friends asked him whether he got depressed about the world. He replied by explaining a little about his Christian faith.

- Arthur has been retired for almost a year. He is gradually getting used to having time on his hands. When the first enthusiasm for retirement had abated, he happened to mention to his minister that he didn't have very much to do. The minister had heard that the local secondary school wanted people to help pupils who had reading difficulties. Why didn't Arthur go in to help? He would only have to listen to them read. Well, Arthur had never worked with young people in his life. His only contact with teenagers was when he complained to the ones at the bus stop outside his house about the crisp packets they dropped in his garden. But he decided to have a go. Now he goes into the school one morning a week and spends two hours listening to pupils read. Arthur would never have believed it possible but he has really enjoyed getting to know them. As for the pupils, they can't get over the fact that an adult not only has time to hear them read but also wants to chat with them.

• On a chilly autumn evening, three people are practising a drama sketch. Usually when they do this it is for a church service, but this time is different. Tomorrow morning they are going to one of the local schools with the youth worker from their church. He is quite often invited into local schools to lead worship, and the other week he decided that the next time this happened he would try to take the church drama group with him. The school was delighted at the idea and, even though some members of the group will be at work, there are enough available to make it possible. It will be a very different kind of audience to the one they are used to, but they are looking forward to the challenge.

• Monday mornings are always hectic, and this one is no better than the rest. Jane, who is head of a year-group as well as a geography teacher, is settling down to some paperwork. There is a knock at the door, and outside Jane finds a girl from her year-group in floods of tears. She takes her in and tries to find out what is wrong. Some of the other girls have upset her, but Jane soon realises that there are other problems underneath. For the next half hour they talk. Lots of issues emerge about the girl's home situation and, although there is nothing Jane can do just then, the simple fact that someone has sensed the bigger problem has helped. Jane sends her back to her class, making a mental note to try to talk to the girl's mother.

For many people schools work means taking assemblies or lessons, that is, public presentation in schools. Thankfully, this is one of the opportunities open to us, but it is only *one* of the possibilities. The stories at the beginning of this chapter are examples of just some of the things Christians are doing in schools. One involves a teacher, one a pupil and the others people from local churches taking the trouble to do something to help. In only two of them is there straightforward talking about the Christian faith, but in each the people are consciously motivated by the fact that they are Christians. Christian work in schools presents many different opportunities, which means that all kinds of people can find something to contribute.

STARTING IN THE RIGHT PLACE

Because there are so many possibilities we need to get our basic thinking about schools work clear. Most of us are pragmatic and want to know what will work. The danger is, however, that we will focus too much on the means rather than the end. Yet the way in which we serve God is more important than the method we use. We need to take as our starting point God's call for each of us to be Christ's ambassadors. As his ambassadors, it is literally as though 'God were making his appeal through us' (2 Cor 5:20).

The fact is that the work of an ambassador involves more than just teaching – it involves lifestyle. When we hear stories of diplomats ignoring traffic laws or not paying fines, it affects our image of their country. All their careful promotional work is undone if they do not act as good citizens abroad. Not surprisingly, sensible ambassadors do all they can to promote the image of their own country by making a positive contribution to the one they are in.

There is an obvious link to schools work. If the way Christians live is as important as what they say, no matter how much Christians from outside are able to do in school, the witness of pupils and teachers who go there each day will be crucial. In the same way, what outsiders do has an impact on this witness, and it is important for visitors to recognise that other Christians will have to bear the consequences of what they do for a long time after.

Jesus described his people as 'the salt of the earth' and 'the light of the world' (Matt 5:13,14). These two ideas neatly describe different aspects of what God has called us to be. Salt brings change, and just a little of it can make a huge difference. Light, meanwhile, exposes the truth. When the light is switched on, you see things as they really are. The examples we looked at earlier show some of the ways in which Christians can be salt and light in school. Arthur, the teacher and the mums in the prayer group were like salt – they were making a tangible difference to people's lives. On the other hand, Simon, the drama group and the youth worker were bringing light into the school – they were explaining aspects of Christian truth. However, their *behaviour* also had the effect of salt. If it did not, then I suspect that their words were pretty ineffective. In the same way, some of those operating at the salt level would have spoken about their Christian faith too at some point. The important thing is to be consistent: what we do must match what we say. Jesus did not allow us the luxury of separating the qualities of salt and light, and giving precedence to one at the expense of the other. The Christian must be both in ways that are appropriate to particular situations.

SCHOOLS WORK FOR ALL

Jesus said that there were no exceptions when it came to being salt and light: 'You *are* the salt . . .', 'You *are* the light . . .' Schools, it seems clear, need both salt and light. Many situations and people in them need change, and the light of truth seems wholly appropriate to a place of education. Therefore, in principle, all Christians can be involved in schools work at one level or another. This leaves each of us facing the question, '*Is* God calling *me* to do something in schools? And, if so, *what* does he want me to do?'

We will probably find the answers by asking a few more questions.

'What are the needs and opportunities?'

For many people an introduction to schools work comes through a specific opportunity. A friend of mine got involved when his local school was desperate for a gardener! Recognising that weeding can be Christian schools work may only come with hindsight! Whatever our way in, we need to be cautious about starting with or imposing our own agenda.

'Is anyone else doing it already?'

The 'Lone Ranger' syndrome is alive and well. It is so easy to think that because *we* have only just seen a need, no one else has seen it before. I was once in a meeting where someone said that there was no Christian work in a particular school. Another person interrupted and pointed out that this was not true: his team had been working there weekly for the past nine years! Do some research before diving in.

'How much time do I have?'

Enthusiasm is great, but be realistic. Serious involvement will take serious time. If you can't make a proper commitment, there are two options: you can make time by dropping something else, or you can recognise that the fact you have seen a need does not necessarily mean you are the best person to meet it.

'When do I have time?'

If the time you are available is in the evening or at weekends, your involvement is not likely to be the same as if you are free during the day. This does not mean you can't do anything, just that you will probably do different things.

Parent Teacher Associations, prayer groups, governors' meetings may all be possible in the evening. On the other hand, Christian groups in schools, collective worship (assemblies) and the like take place in school time.

'What gifts and skills do I have?'
If the thought of speaking to more than two people at once fills you with dread, it is unlikely that God is calling you to offer to lead school worship. (Don't rule it out for the future though!) Again, the fact that you can see a need does not mean you are the person to fill it. At the same time, don't be bashful. You may have skills you are not aware of. Ask for other people's advice – it could be very valuable.

'What experience do I have?'
If you are a former teacher, there may be obvious opportunities for you. However, other experience is useful too. The professional skills of parents may be invaluable. If you have no children, your own experience of school may help, but do recognise that the rate of change in schools is fast and to some extent your experience may be out of date.

'Could I work with someone else?'
If the answer is 'No, because no one else is available', make sure that you really have checked this out. If the answer is 'No, because I find it hard to work with other people', perhaps you should consider whether you want to be involved in this kind of work at all. Individualism is not necessarily helpful: somewhere along the line you will have to co-operate with someone else in schools work.

So far we have looked at schools work from the perspective of an individual taking up opportunities in their local school. We have seen that this ministry is not just for experts. An exciting development of the past few years is that an increasing number of Christian churches and organisations have employed people as schools workers. As this has happened, a number of different models of schools work have developed. Each has its strengths and weaknesses and, whilst I personally have preferences, I recognise that there is no one model that can address all the needs and respond to all the opportunities we face. Likewise, individuals have different gifts, and the work they do rightly has to make use of those gifts.

The speaker/evangelist

For many people this model is probably the one that first springs to mind when they think of schools work. Assemblies or school worship, religious education and voluntary Christian groups present many opportunities to speak to pupils in school. Work and other responsibilities may mean that many people who are gifted with the young are not available during the school day, so it makes sense to employ people who can take up these opportunities. When I taught RE, I was very grateful for the people who came to our school from time to time to do this kind of work. They were a great help.

The strength of this model is, of course, the sheer number of people that one worker can speak to. However, when we consider the thousands of pupils there may be in any particular area, the scale of the task seems enormous. People working in this way often feel frustrated by the lack of opportunity for significant relationships with the young people themselves. One person can take no more than five early morning assemblies in a week. And in secondary schools, where assembly takes place in smaller groups such as year-groups, the contact that any one worker may have with pupils is equally limited, though personal communication may be better.

Indeed, the worker's own gifts may limit his or her effectiveness. Very few people are gifted to work right across the age range. Five-year-olds need a very different approach from those about to leave school! Almost inevitably, therefore, a schools worker will concentrate on a limited age

29

range of pupils. This is obviously sensible but may leave many opportunities untouched.

The 'relational' worker

Traditional Christian youth work has highlighted a major problem in bringing the gospel to young people. How do we reach the ones with whom we have no natural contact? They don't join our groups or come to our meetings, and they don't tend to have Christian friends.

The 'relational' or 'incarnational' approach reverses our common ways of working. Instead of putting on things for people to go to – clubs, groups, events and so on – we go to them. Workers concentrate on building relationships rather than running programmes. This approach has been used in secular youth work in the form of the detached youth worker. The idea of incarnation is a key one in Christian thinking. It follows the example of Christ in its concern to live out the gospel, to meet people where they are, to identify with their pain and suffering.

This approach typically involves a person working in just one school, and there are several examples around the country. Scripture Union has for a number of years had a 'relational' staff worker in Oxford – any activities that he arranges with young people in the area arise out of his relationship with them, and not vice versa.

As well as a single worker, a team of people can also be effective in using the relational approach. It is a challenging one. We may find uncomfortable the task of going out to people who do not particularly want to know us. It requires people who can become skilled in building relationships with individuals who may be very different to them.

The enabler

The reality of schools work is that the opportunities and needs are usually far greater than our ability to meet them. One person is limited not only in time but also in gifts and ability. For this reason many schools workers have seen that a number of tasks are necessary if our ministry in schools is to be effective.

Mobilisation is probably the most important of these. There are many children and young people with whom the church has no contact. Yet, ironically, relative success in youth work can sometimes make it harder for us to see this. Even if we do have contact with lots of young people, the fact is that the vast majority remain unreached.

We do not just need to do more, we need greater diversity in what we do. No single approach – or personality, for that matter – will be effective with everybody. Some kids love being in groups; others will hate it. The youth leader who is adored by one person might be given the cold-shoulder by someone else. And our work in schools needs to take account of this.

Direct evangelism is important, but so too is Christian example. Time and again I have heard people who become Christians after leaving school say that, with hindsight, they realised a particular teacher was a Christian and the witness of this teacher had been one of the things that influenced them, almost without their knowing.

The task of the enabler is to mobilise others who are better placed to respond to the needs and opportunities in schools. From a base of active involvement, this type of worker can pass on the vision, train people, encourage and support Christian teachers and pupils, develop links between schools and churches and have an overview of work in a particular area. In taking this collaborative approach, one person can accomplish a much more far-reaching ministry than he or she could do alone, both in terms of workload and ability.

These three models of locally based schools worker are not, of course, the only possibilities. Many people combine aspects of all three. It is important, however, that we think clearly about what exactly we are trying to achieve. Our thinking will be influenced by the understanding we have of our gifts and the opportunities there are to use them. However, if we are not clear about what we are trying to do, we will probably end up floundering, without any sense of direction.

Local groups
All these models of work are being practised by different people around the country. Alongside them, in a number of areas, local organisations have sprung up to encourage and develop Christian work in schools. Some of these have had the very focused aim of networking Christians who may have different kinds of involvement in their local schools. These include parents, teachers, other education professionals, youth and schools workers, and any Christians with a concern for the world of education. One good example of this kind of group is Christians in Derbyshire Schools (CIDS).

Other groups, such as Ipswich Christian Youth Ministries, have concentrated on the work of full-time schools workers, whilst developing other youth-related ministries with the local churches.

A number of national organisations have schemes that enable local Christians to come together to establish schools work in their area. Scripture Union In Schools has an Associate Worker scheme that links up with local groups to assist them in employing schools workers. The local group or trust has overall responsibility for the project, whilst Scripture Union helps with training and support. Thus the energy and initiative come from the local community, while the schools worker has the advantages that arise from being part of a national team.

National network
One of the most exciting developments of the past few years has been the establishment of the Schools Ministry Network (SMN). SMN is a completely independent body that links a very wide range of people who are involved in schools

ministry. Some of them are members of national organisations, others work with local churches and groups. Individuals have to be recommended by another Network
member to join. Central to SMN is the agreement of all
members to a set of principles and practices in relation to
working in schools (see Appendix, p 139).

The Network reflects the responsible and sensitive way
in which Christian schools workers would like to be seen to
approach their work. Within its first two years of existence
it attracted a membership of well over 300, and its activities
to date have included regular mailings, annual conferences
and involvement in local seminars and consultations.

Christians are recognising the importance of work in
schools as never before. The opportunity is obviously there.
The challenge to us is to respond.

3

MAKING CONTACT WITH SCHOOLS

If churches can be forbidding places to people not used to attending, so can schools. For many adults, going into a school brings back all kinds of strange feelings and memories. During my teaching days I remember watching people at parents' evenings. Parents often seemed more nervous than their children – more nervous even than me. Some of them had bad memories of school. Others found it strange not being in the role of a pupil and had to work hard at being grown-up!

Of course for many adults there is no problem at all. They are used to going in and out of the school their children attend, particularly if it is a primary school. If you are a parent who wants to get more involved in your own children's school, the initial contact is relatively easy because you are already known. In fact you may well be fighting the school off (particularly if it is a primary) rather than trying to persuade them to let you help. When we were choosing a school for our children, one head suggested ways in which we could get involved even before we had decided to send them there.

Nevertheless, there are things to consider if we plan to get involved in visiting the school our own children attend. How do we respond to our children when they see us? We must make sure that we do not undermine their relationship with their teacher. On the other hand, we need to be careful that we don't embarrass them. I sometimes take assembly in my children's school and whilst at the moment they like me going ('That's my dad!'), I realise that it will not always be like that. Already I sense there might be a touch of embarrassment, initially at least. It is impossible to be hard and fast about this because all children are different, but we do need to avoid making life difficult for our children, especially as they get older.

INITIAL CONTACT

If you are employed as a schools worker, there may be no alternative to starting from scratch and introducing yourself to a school. Some people's approach is to send a circular letter to the head teacher explaining that they are in the area and available to help. They sit back and wait for a flood of letters and phone calls. Unfortunately, the flood is more likely to be a trickle if there's any response at all.

A much better alternative to sending a letter out of the blue is to find someone who will introduce you. It might be a teacher in the school, or possibly a parent. A local minister or church leader may already have good contact and be willing to help, or perhaps the head of another school will say something on your behalf. Often there is a good local grapevine amongst heads anyway, and you may already be known. Of course this can work negatively as sell as positively!

Notwithstanding what I have just said, there is sometimes a place for sending letters. A general letter of introduction can be a useful way of getting your name or organisation known. You might decide to follow the example of some charity fund-raisers and write to say you will be phoning later – phone calls out of the blue can be even worse than letters. The important thing is to be realistic and to recognise that you are not likely to get a reply unless the letter is very personal and specific (rather than part of a mass mailing). Do be certain that you have the right name for the person you are writing to, and spell it correctly. A phone call to the school secretary is the simple way to ensure this. It is really a question of professionalism: sending a letter to the last-but-one head and spelling their name wrong will not do much for your image. Of course the 'what can go wrong will go wrong' law still applies, and if you are sending out more than one letter at a time, double-check that you have the correct name attached to the correct school and the right letter in the right envelope. The chances of you getting it wrong, inadvertently changing the person's sex and sending it to their greatest rival are probably greater than winning the lottery!

It goes without staying that the letter itself is crucial. If you are not careful, you may communicate more than you intend. Headed note paper can be a blessing or a curse, so if you have any control over its design ask yourself how a head teacher receiving a letter on it would respond. At all costs, avoid anything like the one a colleague produced as a 'how not to' exercise, which was headed 'Judgement and Glory: Messages for the End Times'. Head teachers are a very different audience from potential supporters in a local church.

Correct spelling and punctuation are important, so if you are not confident in this area get someone else to check the letter for you. (Don't rely on computer spell-checks!) Make sure that the printing is good, and avoid that old, worn dot-matrix effort! Most business letters look as good as a quality book did ten years ago, and this is the standard many people expect.

When it comes to content, start by trying to put yourself in the position of a head who is not very sympathetic to Christians. What would you be looking for? What would make you cringe? It is important to write as a professional to a professional – long and flowery is out. Try to be friendly without being too informal. Your letter will be one of many that the head has to deal with, so have a clear idea of what you want to say and express it as concisely as you can. If the letter is simply to introduce yourself, say that. If you have a request, such as an appointment to meet, make that plain.

You do not want the response to your letter to be a puzzled 'Huh?'

Don't assume that the person you are writing to will know anything about you or the local church scene. They may have no idea what a schools worker is. Most of the people and organisations respected by Christians are totally unknown to anyone outside the church, so dropping such names may well reinforce the impression that Christians are out of touch with the real world.

Finally, two prejudices of mine when it comes to this kind of letter. First, don't sign off with anything like 'Love in Jesus'. And second, please, please, please no little kisses, hearts or flowers after your signature. Just think of this person as the head teacher you had when you were at school . . .

JUST VISITING

If you are arranging a meeting with a head teacher, again, do put yourself in their shoes. Time is always tight and heads have many people making demands upon them. See a meeting as a privilege rather than a right, and don't be surprised if the head is a little suspicious. They may rightly wonder what you are about. Try to go alone or possibly with one other person. Any more can look like a foreign delegation and appear quite threatening ('This is Bishop X, here is Elder Y and over there is Apostle Z, meanwhile our Director will be with us in a moment . . .').

Schools are often surprisingly open buildings and it can be relatively easy to wander around them. All the same, don't give in to the temptation. Strangers roaming around a school rightly create suspicion – would you want strangers drifting into your children's school? Always go the main office and introduce yourself, unless someone in the school has specifically told you otherwise. Even if a teacher does arrange to meet you in the classroom, check whether you still ought to go to the office – the teacher may be assuming that you will do that anyway.

In some cases, the office may not be too easy to find! Schools are often a hotchpotch of buildings, and the office that was at the front when the school was first built may now be somewhere inside a labyrinth. You need to to allow a little extra time if you have an appointment at a school that is unfamiliar to you.

The school secretary is one of your key contacts. The secretary and the caretaker are often the people who really know what is happening in a school. If they want to, they can be very effective in stopping you actually making contact with the person you want to see, so treat them well. Very often in the secretary's office you will find yourself in a little crowd of pupils sorting out dinner money, forms and the like, with teachers rushing in to collect registers or make phone calls, so don't be surprised if the person behind the desk seems a little hassled. You may even for a moment be mistaken for a pupil!

A school is a very busy place with many short-term deadlines, and things only work well when people keep to them. This may mean that the head can only see you at a very specific time. Even then there may be interruptions and not much time for small talk. It is very important to read the situation well and not outstay your welcome. On the other hand, some heads will appreciate the chance to talk to someone from outside, so you may find yourself chatting away for ages. I remember feeling embarrassed as a very youthful schools worker when I sat in the office of one head whom I'd never met before and he proceeded to tell me all kinds of things about the school that it was not my place to know! Discretion is the name of the game.

It is important to have a clear idea of the purpose of your visit if it is more than just a courtesy call. The head, or whoever you are meeting, is bound to say at some point, 'And what can I do for you?' I know this seems obvious, but it is important not to give the impression you have plans that you simply want the school to rubber-stamp. So don't say, 'I was wondering when I could bring our drama group to your assembly.' Talk first about the fact that you are keen to help the school in some way. This may lead to a discussion about what you can offer, but your ideas will have been negotiated and you won't leave the teacher feeling that something has been imposed. After all, it is their school.

There is a delicate balance between offering to help and having a clear proposal. We need to be honest about our motives. Are we really serious about serving the school? The test comes when the school is not interested in our idea but has an alternative suggestion. It often grates on me when people speak about 'getting into school'. I know what they mean and their motives are often excellent, but the phrase seems to suggest confrontation rather than co-operation, almost as though they were going into the school against its wishes.

It is useful to look at things from a long-term perspective as this will help us to focus on the needs of the school rather than our own ideas. A wise head will want to get to know you better before involving you more in the school. So you may be asked to do something that is low-risk from the school's point of view, or put in touch with the school's Christian group or a teacher who needs some voluntary help. This doesn't necessarily mean you are being fobbed off; remember – the head has to answer to staff and parents if you turn out to be a problem. The fact that a head is cautious can work to your advantage.

The important thing to remember at this stage is that you are trying to build a relationship. You are making an investment in the future, and getting things wrong at this point may make things much more difficult further down the track.

BEING THERE

As a result of your meeting, you may be invited to visit the school again. You might take part in assembly or visit the school's Christian group, find yourself helping with a sports team or assisting in a classroom. So, what now?

We are representing Christ in school and what we do speaks as loudly as what we say, so Paul's advice is highly appropriate: 'conduct yourselves in a manner worthy of the gospel of Christ' (Phil 1:27). Essential always is courtesy. When we go into a school, we go as visitors and therefore should wait to be invited to do things. We are there to serve, not to be served, so it is not a good idea to go around insisting on our rights, even if we feel that we are not being well treated. The people looking after us are probably being pulled in several directions at once, so we need to be understanding if they get distracted, and prepared to wait patiently for them to get to know and trust us. I have had some very embarrassing experiences when I have taken people to schools (often musicians, unfortunately) who have gone with the idea that they are somehow doing the school a favour. They have insisted on rooms being changed, equipment moved, and so on, with no recognition of the problems they are creating. The more hassle we give a school, the less likely we are to be welcomed back.

Teachers are often very sensitive to noise levels. They are usually working hard at getting the pupils to be reasonably quiet, so to have visitors crashing around whilst lessons are going on is no help at all. Likewise, visitors can be quite an attraction to pupils. It's great when they greet you in the corridor and want to be friendly, but be aware of the problems this can create for the school. Be friendly too, but don't create a following, especially after lessons have started. It is easy enough to remind pupils that it is time they were back in class.

Dress is still an issue in many schools, and this can make things difficult for a visitor. In some schools, staff dress quite formally – jackets and ties for men, skirts and dresses but definitely no trousers for women – but in other places it seems that anything goes. A good principle is invisibility. We probably don't want to be remembered for our stunning wardrobe, so an attempt at camouflage (not military gear, though . . .) is a reasonable idea. You can always ask a teacher what is acceptable, or just notice what the teachers are wearing. I once made the mistake of assuming what a school would be like, turned up in a pullover and tie, and felt very out of place because the men were all wearing suits and academic gowns. The strange thing is that pupils can often have a very conservative idea of what a visitor should wear (after all, they may be wearing a uniform they don't like) and assume that someone who dresses very differently is posing.

Showing an interest in the school is very important. Ask questions, take notice of what is going on and don't be too preoccupied with what you are there to do (although this is hard if you are terrified!). Most teachers identify very strongly with their schools, so they may be very conscious of the impression you are taking away. It may sometimes seem that they are more concerned that you are impressed than that you do a good job with their pupils. A few positive comments such as 'Oh, I thought they were very good' can be very helpful when a teacher is apologising to you about pupils' behaviour (provided that it is true, of course!).

At the same time, we need to be careful about what we say, especially about other schools. Comparisons are often not helpful, and the most positive comment can be misheard or misunderstood. Likewise, we must think before we make critical comments. It is inevitable that we will see things and make judgements about schools, but we must be discreet about expressing these. It is easy to fall into the trap of saying unhelpful things about a school when we are away from it. People may want to know what we think of certain schools and we need to be judicious in our response. We are not inspectors, we are friends, and our role at this stage is to support not criticise. So watch what you say – words have an amazing way of coming back to haunt us.

Perhaps the most important outcome is that we leave the school thinking of us as a friend. All kinds of people visit schools for all kinds of reasons, many of them official; but we have the advantage that we go with no official 'clout'.

We go to serve God through serving the school and this gives us the freedom of friendship, not just with the school as an institution but with the young people and adults for whom it exists.

SUMMARY

- Personal introductions are best. Who do you know?

- Letters should be:
    personal – use the person's name
    professional – spelling and grammar matter
    specific – be clear about the response you want

- Phone calls are best preceded by a letter if it is your first contact with the school.

- Visits:
    arrive on time
    don't take a delegation
    go to the school office first
    remember – schools are busy places
    go with specific ideas, but be flexible
    always take the long-term perspective

- While you are in school:
    courtesy matters
    try not to be a disruption
    dress appropriately
    show interest in the school as a whole
    aim to make friends with the school

4

'AM I ALLOWED TO . . .?'

A team of evangelists visited a school to speak in assembly. They were not used to working in schools, but this seemed to be a great opportunity for the pupils to hear the gospel. To the best of their knowledge they were the first Christians to visit the school for years. They knew that they were not likely to be in the area again for some time and wanted to make the most of the opportunity. As far as the pupils were concerned it was great. For one thing, they liked the music. And when one of the visitors spoke convincingly about the difference that Christ had made to her life, you could have heard a pin drop. When she finished speaking, the leader stood up and asked anyone who wanted to commit their life to Christ, to come to the front of the hall. In the silence, twenty or thirty pupils walked hesitantly to the front.

It was several years later, long after the head teacher had left, that any other Christians were invited to visit the school . . .

These evangelists may have meant well but their action effectively closed the school to Christian visitors. School is a different kind of territory to that in which many of us are used to working. Whether we like it or not, we have to work in ways that are appropriate to the nature and environment of a school.

What is it about schools that means we have to be so careful? First, schools operate within a legal framework. They are not free agents able to do whatever they wish, and anyone from outside needs to be aware of the requirements the school has to meet.

However, as well as these legal obligations, schools have a responsibility to the parents or guardians of the children in their care. This is made even more significant by the fact that education is compulsory. Whilst in theory unhappy parents can move their children to a different school, they really have very few options. The school rightly, then, has to take very seriously the wishes and concerns of parents.

WHAT ABOUT THE LAW?

Strictly speaking, the law has very little to say to visitors coming into a school whether they be Christian, Moslem, Sikh or whatever. The head teacher and the governors of a school are the people to whom the law is addressed – they are the ones who carry the can. We need to appreciate this fully. Any involvement you may have in a school is by permission, not by right. There is no need in trying to insist that a head allows you to visit a school. If head teachers do not want you, they do not have to have you.

Nevertheless, in Britain the law has very specific expectations of schools when it comes to religion. Religious education (RE) and collective worship are, like many aspects of school life, governed by various Acts of Parliament. In England and Wales, the key ones are the Education Act 1944, the Education Reform Act 1988 and the Education Act 1993. The requirement of these Acts regarding religious education and collective worship are explained in the Department For Education Circular No. 1/94, and for Wales in the Welsh Office Circular 10/94.

Scotland has different provisions – primary schools are only required to provide an act of worship once a week and secondary schools once a month. National guidelines were published in 1992, and these are implemented through regional arrangements. Likewise, in Northern Ireland all grant-aided schools, other than special schools or nursery schools, are required to hold a daily act of collective worship. Both worship and religious education are Christian but not denominational.

Let's take the situation in England and Wales as an example, to draw attention to some of the considerations that lie behind what schools do. This is not a complete statement of the legal position! It applies to all 'maintained' (ie government-funded) schools, including those that are grant-maintained. There are one or two differences as far as denominational voluntary-aided and voluntary-controlled schools are concerned, but these will be mentioned when we get to them.

The overall responsibility of a school

Regarding the spiritual needs of pupils, the school's responsibility goes further than the obviously religious parts of school life. The curriculum should promote 'the spiritual, moral, cultural, mental and physical development of pupils at the school and of society'. Not only that, pupils should be prepared for the 'opportunities, responsibilities and experiences of adult life' (Education Reform Act 1988).

Religious education

• This must be open to all pupils, including sixth-formers.

• Sixth-form colleges in the further education sector must also provide RE (Further and Higher Education Act 1992, Section 45).

• RE 'should seek: to develop pupils' knowledge, understanding and awareness of Christianity, as the predominant religion in Great Britain, and other principal religions represented in the country; to encourage respect for those holding different beliefs; and to help to promote pupils' spiritual, moral, cultural and mental development' (Department For Education Circular No. 1/94, paragraph 16).

• In county schools, voluntary-controlled schools and grant-maintained schools that were formerly county schools, religious education must be non-denominational.

It may, however, include teaching about denominational differences.

• In voluntary-aided schools, the RE offered is determined by the governors in accordance with the denominational basis of the school.

• Parents have the right to withdraw their children from RE.

• There is no statutory amount of time that a school has to allocate to RE, but it should be a 'reasonable time', allowing 'sufficient rigour and depth' (DFE Circ No. 1/94, para 39).

• There are safeguards for teachers who do not wish to participate in RE unless they are specifically employed to teach it.

Collective worship

• All schools must provide a daily act of collective worship for all pupils.

• Sixth-form colleges in the further education sector must hold an act of collective worship on at least one day a week, which students *may* attend (Further and Higher Education Act 1992, Section 44).

• Collective worship is not the same as an 'assembly' which is purely to provide a forum for matters of school administration, making announcements, and so on.

• Collective worship 'should aim to provide the opportunity for pupils to worship God, to consider spiritual and moral issues and to explore their own beliefs; to encourage participation and response, through listening to and joining in the worship offered; and to develop community spirit, promote a common ethos and shared values, and reinforce positive attitudes' (DFE Circ No. 1/94, para 50).

• The 'majority of acts of worship over a term must be wholly or mainly of a broadly Christian character' (DFE Circ No. 1/94, para 62).

• In county schools, collective worship should not 'be distinctive of any particular Christian denomination' (DFE Circ No. 1/94, para 61).

- Parents have the right to withdraw their children from collective worship.
- Teachers have the right to withdraw from collective worship but may be required to take part in a non-religious assembly.
- If the make-up of a school is such that Christian worship would be inappropriate, the head may apply to the Standing Advisory Council for Religious Education (SACRE) for a determination that this requirement should not apply to the whole school or to a particular category of pupil.

In addition to all the above, there are two statements in Circular No. 1/94 that are directly relevant to outside visitors. Both of them concern how a head teacher can ensure that the law regarding collective worship is fulfilled, even if there are insufficient staff members willing to lead it.

The first says that, in finding people from the local community, head teachers should take account of 'a person's ability to conduct such an act of worship for pupils of the family background, ages and aptitudes concerned' (DFE Circ No. 1/94, para 147). Enthusiasm is not enough: visitors need to be appropriate for the particular situation.

The second statement relates to the school's responsibility for pupils: 'nothing overrides the school's responsibility in relation to the health and safety of pupils. Head teachers will wish, for example, to consider the need for the presence of a member of staff at acts of worship being led by individuals from outside the school' (DFE Circ No. 1/94, para 149). Most of the time this issue will not arise because a teacher will be present, but it is worth remembering that schools have this particular responsibility and cannot pass it over to a visitor.

Clearly, what the law says is addressed to schools, not visitors. Nevertheless, as visitors we do need to understand the framework within which a school has to work, and a number of significant principles are clear. The first is that the spiritual and moral development of pupils is not just the province of RE and collective worship. It has a place in the curriculum as a whole.

Another principle relates to denominationalism. Whilst RE and collective worship are to reflect the Christian tradition of the country, they are not to be denominational unless the school is a denominational one. This may well mean that a school is rightly cautious about appearing to be too closely linked with one particular church. Interdenominational approaches are very helpful in this respect.

Finally, freedom of conscience is reflected in the legal position. Both pupils (through their parents) and teachers have the right to withdraw from RE and collective worship. The law recognises both the diversity of the community and the freedom of the individual.

This, then, is the kind of legal framework within which schools have to work with regard to religion. As outsiders we may sometimes feel a little bewildered by what a school does and does not do, but at the end of the day it is the head teacher who is responsible for ensuring that the school complies with the law.

WHAT IS RIGHT?

As we saw before, compliance with the law is not the only concern of a school. It rightly has to consider the parents of its pupils – the school is answerable to them for what it does with their children. This becomes increasingly difficult as society gets more complex. Different social, religious and cultural backgrounds make it increasingly difficult to find agreement on many issues, even relatively simple ones. Look at the arguments that blow up from time to time about school uniform or haircuts. So it is not surprising that when it comes to religion and values, school authorities often feel they are walking through a minefield.

This is the world we are entering when we get involved in schools. The least we can do is to try to understand it from the school's perspective.

Understand the nature of schools

Schools are primarily about education. They are not fishing grounds for eager Christians. This is not to say that there is no place for the gospel in school, but it does mean we need to present it in the context of the educational task of the school. This challenges us to find points at which the Christian faith and what goes on in school intersect. These intersections are not hard to find, because all truth is God's truth. God is not confined to the 'religious bit' of life. Some colleagues and I once visited a school for a week during which we spoke in consumer education, careers, social studies, English – but not RE! The fascinating thing was finding how many natural points of contact those subjects had with the gospel. What we were doing made sense educationally – we were genuinely helping the school in its task – but we were bringing a dimension to the study of a number of subjects, which would probably not otherwise have been present.

One of the key tasks of education is to teach children to test and evaluate ideas, and a consequence of this is that we must be open to challenge. As Christians we want pupils to be able to discern the difference between true and false, good and bad. In practice, this means we will have to be ready to back up our arguments with reasons and evidence. 'Because I say so' will never be adequate. I once heard a schools worker enthuse about the fact that many scientists are Christians. The response of one person in the group was to ask him to name some. It was a reasonable request!

Understand your role in the school

As visitors we do not speak on behalf of the school, we speak as ourselves, as Christians. This is a freedom, not a restriction! It is perfectly justifiable educationally for pupils to hear from Christians about their faith. And because sharing this is the reason for our being there, provided we do it in the right way there should be no grounds for complaint.

What is the right way? When, as Christians, we visit a school, we are like goldfish in a bowl, exposed to view with nowhere to hide. We open ourselves to questions. We can be challenged about why we believe certain things. We can expect people to express different opinions.

Of course, we don't necessarily speak on behalf of *all* Christians. As well as the things which Christians have in common, there are things on which we disagree. It is wise to recognise this in what we say. We don't have to explain every point of view, but we can say that we realise not all Christians think the way we do. The more controversial our ideas are amongst Christians, the more important it is to affirm those other points of view.

Think ahead

It is worth remembering that in school we have at least three audiences watching and listening to us. The pupils, obviously, are one, teachers are another, and parents, indirectly, are a third. Pupils will often talk to parents about what we do and say, and not always accurately, as any teacher will tell you!

Many of the situations that get Christians into hot water in school occur because they have forgotten one or more of those audiences. What do you do when a pupil is talking to you about a deep and meaningful problem and the bell for the next has lesson has gone? What do you say in a RE lesson to the twelve-year-old who asks, 'Does that mean that my grandad is going to hell?' How do you respond to the child who asks if sex outside marriage is wrong, then follows your answer by telling you about his father's girlfriend? Pupils, teachers and parents will have different perspectives on those situations, especially if they are misreported ('I hope grandad's feeling better, Mum, because that woman we had in RE said he's going to hell').

It makes sense to think ahead about how you might deal with some of those situations. Remember, it is perfectly appropriate for you to express the Christian point of view.

Indeed, if you don't express it, you will be failing to do the very thing you are there for. But do remember too that what you say is not necessarily what people will hear. Think carefully!

Watch your language

The way in which we say something can be as important as what we say. In schools in particular, style is all-important. Here are a number of ways of saying the same thing:

'We are all sinners.'
This is blunt, assumes that people understand the word 'sin' and may make people file us away under 'Bible-basher' and stop listening.

'As a Christian, I believe that we are all sinners.'
'As a Christian' recognises that not everyone will agree with us, but it still assumes that people understand what is meant by 'sin'.

'As a Christian, I believe that however good we seem to be, none of us can keep God's laws completely. Have you noticed how everybody seems to fail at some point?'
This is lengthy but explains what sin means and says that we can all see this from our own experience. It invites people to agree with us.

If we want people to hear what we say and not what they think we say, we have to pay attention to the words we use. 'Non-presumptive' language recognises that not everyone will agree with us and that we are ready to justify what we say. When we use it, we are not saying that truth is relative, or that it doesn't matter what you believe. No matter how true something is, people can and will disagree with it!

Here are some examples of non-presumptive language that can keep people ready to listen to us:

'Christians believe that . . .'
'It seems to me . . .'
 The Bible says . . .'
'I think . . .'
'In my experience . . .'
'Would you agree that . . .?'
'I believe . . .'

Put yourself in other people's shoes

A good test of whether we are acting appropriately in school is to try to see things from the other side. How would I feel as a Christian parent if, say, a Hindu speaker came to my child's school? What would I be happy for the visitor to do? What would I be unhappy with?

If it was my children's school, I would be concerned about *how* that person did things. Obviously, children are going to come across new ideas in school – that's what schools are about! But I would not want those ideas to be presented in a way that either assumed my child shared them or excluded the possibility of them being questioned. Likewise, I would not want want my child to be put in the position of having to participate in (as opposed to observe) worship of another faith. I would expect the school to ensure that this visitor understood the concerns of parents like myself and acted appropriately.

Now, if this is what I want for myself, it is reasonable that the children of people who don't share my Christian faith should be treated in the same way. So in school we should recognise in our use of language that not all children or their parents will share our beliefs. Likewise, we must always be open to questioning and not become upset when things get hot! When we speak in schools we are in a privileged situation – parents have little real choice about their children being there and the pupils themselves even less! It is up to us to ensure that we do not abuse this privilege.

SUMMARY

- Be supportive of the school in its legal responsibilities.

- Always remember that schools are places of education.

- Speak as a Christian, but do this in an appropriate way.

- Be sensitive when you are talking about things on which there are genuine disagreements amongst Christians.

- Think about:
      how pupils may react
      how teachers may react
      how parents/guardians may react when you are quoted
         at home

- Choose your words carefully – there will probably be people in your audience who are not Christians.

- Put yourself in the shoes of people who are not Christians.

5

LINKING CHURCH AND SCHOOL

Schools are more open to the outside world than ever before. Most have come a long way since the days of signs saying 'No parents past this point', and it is now not only parents who are welcome. Schools are very aware of their place in society and positively encourage contact with all kinds of community organisations, and this should include churches.

So how can a church develop a practical concern for its local schools? Sometimes concern exists out of necessity: a church has its own voluntary-aided or voluntary-controlled school and cannot escape its responsibilities. In other churches, the fact that there are so many families with school-aged children or teachers in the congregation means that schools naturally become a concern. Unfortunately, neither of those factors ensures that a church will take the opportunity of schools seriously.

GETTING SCHOOLS ONTO THE AGENDA

For anything to happen, school has to get onto the agenda of the church in a significant way. In one church, a parent 'banged the drum' of involvement in schools for several years before the rest of the congregation took notice and considered what they could do. In another, it was the discovery that some parents were very concerned about their children's RE lessons that led the church to commit itself to pray regularly for local schools. The appointment of a youth and families worker, who recognised the need to base his work within the community, formed the beginnings of the relationship between another church and the schools in their area. And when the (non-Christian) head teacher of a secondary school asked a minister to help with counselling some pupils, the congregation realised that here was something they could be involved in.

Raising a church's awareness of schools is often a slow-drip process, so patience is needed as well as vision. For many adults, school has not been part of their daily experience for a long time and has changed a great deal since they were there. Getting people who are currently involved in schools to speak in a church meeting is one way of beginning to bring people up to date and helping them see the possibilities. Many churches use Education Sunday to raise the profile of schools. One arranged a Sunday afternoon tea when teachers and young people in the congregation talked to the rest of the church about their school. They discussed the opportunities and problems they experienced as Christians each day, and the afternoon ended with prayer in groups for each school.

THE QUESTION WHY?

Getting schools onto the church's agenda is, of course, only the start: we want it to lead to real involvement with schools. However, it is important at this stage for us to examine our motives. We need to ask *why* we want to get involved. Is it because we see the school as providing us with a platform of some kind? Or do we want to be there for the long haul, serving Christ by serving the school? All too often a church has looked at contact with schools purely in terms of what *it* wants to get out of the relationship; the agenda has been to get an evangelist or speaker into the school, then leave the school in peace until the next time there is a visiting evangelist. This sort of approach is often unintentional, but usually comes about because we have not thought through the issues surrounding schools work. Nevertheless, we must give time to do this thinking. Most head teachers have a sophisticated detection system that quickly establishes the motives of people wanting access to their pupils!

The idea of Christian service provides a good basis for a church's work in schools. Jesus himself said that he 'did not come to be served, but to serve' (Matt 20:28). Looking at schools from this perspective can unleash a lot of creativity and enable us to minister effectively in what are crucial centres of the community.

As with any outside visitor, a good starting point for a church is to ask what a school needs and then look at what it can offer. Apart from anything else this ensures that we work with the real needs rather than the ones that we imagine exist. But how do we find out? The obvious way is to ask! Most head teachers will respond well to a group from the community offering to help, and may even have some immediate specific needs. At the same time, it is good to have an idea of the kinds of things that you might be able to offer. Let's look at some ways in which churches can make a positive contribution to schools.

PRAYER

The most important thing a church can give to anyone is prayer. It goes without saying that we should be praying for Christians in schools, and there is more on that elsewhere in this book. But what about prayer for the school as a whole? Everyone in the school community has needs; we need to pray for these and about the issues facing the school as an institution. In fact, most people are quite keen to be prayed for, even if they are not too sure about prayer themselves. The 'say one for me!' attitude still exists. Some will see the offer of prayer as a gift – a welcome balance to the impression that the church is always asking for things.

Prayer groups

An effective way to pray regularly for schools is in prayer groups. Some groups may consist mainly of parents and focus on a particular school. Others may be church- or area-based and concentrate on a number of schools. In one area I know, groups occasionally come together to pray for groups of schools, usually secondary schools and their feeder primaries.

Getting started

Most prayer groups seem to start by someone saying, 'Why don't we pray?' Obviously, a few parents who know each other don't need a massive publicity campaign to get a group off the ground. On the other hand, it is very easy for groups that start in this way to look like cliques, particularly if their members are all from the same church. If you become involved in this kind of group, it would be wise to make it as widely known as possible. Advertise it in local churches as well as in schools if possible. You might be surprised at some of the people who commit themselves to prayer.

It is important to inform the school of your plans. Make sure you communicate with the head teacher as soon as possible, otherwise he or she might get the wrong idea and imagine all kinds of subversive things are going on!

It is also important to be well prepared. Obviously, you are not there to ask permission – prayer is one of the few things that no one can stop! Nevertheless, it is good in terms of your relationship with the school to be as positive as possible, and a courtesy call will probably pay dividends. Adopt a similar approach to that outlined in chapter three and work out what you want to say beforehand, trying to put yourself in the head teacher's shoes. What would you want to know about a prayer group? Probably, at least, the purpose of the group and who is behind it. Good answers and a positive rather than defensive attitude will, more often than not, get a favourable response. After all, even schools need all the support they can get!

Do not be afraid to ask for help in publicising your group. Explain that you want it to be open to everyone and you would appreciate the chance to advertise it in school or even in a bulletin to parents. Many if not most head teachers will be co-operative, and the worst they can do is say no!

One band of Christians went to see the head about starting a prayer group in a state of some trepidation. After listening to their plan, she said that she thought it was a good idea, offered to advertise it in the school bulletin, gave them two or three current things to pray for and went on to spend some time talking about her personal needs. It was rather more than they expected!

Making it happen

There is no best way to run a group. It all depends on who is involved and their particular circumstances. Some groups meet during the day, others in the evening. The frequency of meetings varies from weekly to termly to occasionally. In many ways a varied pattern is helpful as it allows the maximum number of people to be involved at one time or another. If meetings are always during the day, working parents are excluded. On the other hand, evening meetings may not be convenient for people with small children.

Prayer groups often include people from a range of churches, so take this into account in the way meetings are run. If you sing, remember that probably not everyone will know the same songs. Open prayer might be a new experience for some – give permission for people to pray silently too. It only takes a little thought to ensure that all kinds of people can feel a part of the group, but it is worth it. A wide range of people serving God together through a prayer group is a positive statement to those who see the church as divided.

Topics for prayer will obviously arise naturally from people's knowledge of the school. All the same, it is good to ask for suggestions. When trust has been established, schools will often given you particular requests. If Christians on the staff cannot get to meetings regularly, don't forget to ask them for ideas; they will probably be glad to make suggestions. Some groups I know of have sent an open invitation to meetings to staff from the school and have received a positive response. One has even arranged occasional lunches for staff as a way of strengthening their relationship. Another way of extending the work of a prayer group is through a simple photocopied sheet of prayer items – a take-away item for people in the meeting, and a way of including those who cannot attend.

Given the kinds of things about which you are likely to pray, remember that confidentiality is vital: prayer should never be a cloak for gossip. It is worth mentioning this as new people come into the group.

Prayer is hard work, and it is easy to get discouraged. On the other hand, we are encouraged to go on when we sense that our prayer is being effective. Some groups find it helpful to keep a record of the things they have prayed for.

Prayer in churches

Much of what we have said about prayer groups applies to churches. Many churches pray regularly for different aspects of the local community, and schools should be a part of this. I recently passed a church that had a sign outside saying, 'This week we are praying for . . .' When I was there, they were praying for the fire brigade, but it could just as easily have been education or a particular school. If we believe in prayer, why shouldn't we let people know what we are praying for?

So, it is good to include intercession for schools within our Sunday worship, and perhaps also our home or cell groups. Some churches produce a weekly prayer bulletin, including the names of schools, of people from the church who work in or have other significant connections with them, or of those who take part in specific activities going on in them, such as school Christian groups.

WHAT WE CAN OFFER

Despite what we may feel, churches have a great deal to offer schools. With a spirit of generosity we can make a significant contribution to their life. Yet, as before, we must be aware of our motives in doing so. Perhaps the real test of the quality of Christian concern for schools is the way in which we respond when there is no apparent benefit to us.

People

Clearly, since churches are communities, people are the main asset we have to offer schools. School worship and religious education are obvious places where churches can provide help, but, as we have seen, there are many other ways in which Christians can be directly involved in schools (see chapters three and four). The value of this is much more than Christians being seen to be helpful, although even that is no bad thing! In getting involved, we build relationships with pupils and staff, and are able to demonstrate the gospel in action.

From the point of view of a church, we need to start with the members of the congregation who are already in schools. There is no point in trying to involve new people if we are not supporting those who are already there. It is important to recognise that what they are doing is a valid part of their Christian ministry. To see the things that people do outside the church as part of the church's ministry can be an exciting development for a congregation. Even though our church organisations may be reaching only a few young people in the area, our church may have a much greater impact on them than we realise because someone in the congregation is teaching in a school.

One important way in which a church can have an impact on schools is through supporting Christians who are school governors. Over the past few years this position has become much more significant. It is a demanding and responsible task that presents Christians with a real opportunity to have a significant and positive influence upon education. However, the nature of the role is such that it demands a lot of time, and the prayer and practical support of the church is vital. So, the person who is a governor may become the one being prayed for in the prayer meeting rather than the one doing the praying!

Of course, this is only the start, and there is a great deal more people could be doing. Education involves people, and schools always need extra pairs of hands. One of the frustration of teachers is that their time is so thinly spread amongst their pupils. A forty-minute lesson provides for barely one minute's individual contact between the teacher and each pupil, even if there is virtually no time with the class as a whole. This is particularly important when it comes to reading, which demands intensive teacher-pupil contact. Not surprisingly then, many schools welcome people from outside coming in, say, to help listen to pupils read, and not only primary schools. One minister was asked by a secondary school if there was anyone in his church who could assist pupils who needed special reading help. He asked a retired couple, who had never done any youth work before, if they would consider doing this. In trepidation, they agreed to have a go. They discovered that, despite all they had thought, they could relate to the pupils. More than that, the pupils appreciated having grandparent figures. The school was delighted with their help.

School trips and camps need extra staffing that teachers are not always able to supply themselves. Many schools ask parents, but there are other people in churches who could be involved too. Church youth workers often have appropriate skills. It may be difficult for a school to provide 'out of school' activities without extra help – sports coaching, music tuition, teaching a craft or skill, or simply 'crowd control' for an activity run by someone else.

Indeed, there are specialist areas where churches are particularly well placed to help. One school had a year-group that had been badly affected by a number of bereavements. Over a period of twelve months, five people had died who were well-known to the pupils, including a teacher, a fellow-pupil and an ex-pupil who was killed in an accident. Over a period of time it became clear to the school that the year-group were not coping. One of the local ministers already knew these pupils quite well through other activities, so the school asked him to provide counselling to help the pupils deal with their loss. As part of this programme he arranged a seminar, taken by a Christian group from outside the area, in the nearby church hall. This provided a more relaxed environment than the school, and the church put on a barbecue lunch for them! At a very difficult time in their lives, these pupils received a positive experience of Christian caring.

Many people in churches have specialist knowledge as a part of their training. Their expertise can be useful in all kinds of curriculum subjects. Nurses and doctors, for example, can contribute to sex education and science subjects as well as RE. However, pupils also benefit from going outside school to gain work experience, and often Christian people in different areas of work can help. In fact a church may itself be able to take someone on work experience in the church office or in some other activity.

School communities often have very practical needs. One was desperate for help in keeping the school gardens under control because it could no longer afford to employ a gardener. It was a great opportunity for someone from one of the local churches. In another school, some local Christians set up and operated a shop selling second-hand school clothing, which met a significant need.

There is one more important area where churches can provide people to help in schools, and that is through parents. Parent Teacher Associations, fund-raising groups and the like all depend upon strong support from parents. By encouraging Christian parents to get involved (and perhaps by helping parents practically through baby-sitting, and so on), we can strengthen Christian involvement in schools.

Resources

Churches have access to many other resources besides people that are useful to schools. Buildings are an obvious starting point. For many schools the most significant contact they have with a local church is borrowing the church building for a carol service. It may not seem very significant (unless you are the person who has to clear up afterwards!) yet it can be a worthwhile contact with both teachers and pupils. We will come back to look at other ways in which church buildings can be an asset.

One of the reasons why schools sometimes struggle with RE is a lack of resources. Whatever we may think of the rightness of this situation (and it is something that we may want to raise with local MPs), it is one we can help to alleviate. Many churches or groups of parents have bought class sets of Bibles for local schools, helped by the special prices available from the Bible Society.

School libraries also value gifts of appropriate books. Christian books are an obvious starting point, but it is worth considering offering other good literature, videos, and so on. The important thing is to offer things of quality. A gift of the old pew Bibles from church will probably convey the wrong message!

One church has made a simple commercial deal with a secondary school in its area. Each year it makes a substantial cash donation to the school, which is used for the development of science laboratories. In return, the church is given the use of one of the school minibuses at weekends and during holidays. Both parties benefit, and a resource is well used.

Often it is knowledge, contacts and expertise that a church can contribute. For a start, there is the obvious religious expertise which church leaders have. Providing lively collective worship on a daily basis can be a major task for schools. One clergyman has gone further than merely making himself available to 'take assembly'. Each week he produces a simple photocopied bulletin containing themes,

Bible passages, music suggestions and other creative ideas for school worship, which he sends to local schools. They are so popular that many schools outside the area are now subscribing!

Information is a crucial commodity these days and is something that can be passed on to schools. Often teachers simply do not know of the books and videos available to help them, particularly for RE and worship. Local churches can provide a useful service just by keeping teachers in touch with resource material, and some Christian book-shops arrange regular resource evenings for teachers.

Charitable trusts are another area of which churches may have knowledge that they can pass on to schools. There are many national and local trusts – often closely connected with the church – that can assist both schools and individual pupils. You could well be the one to discover sources of funding for your local schools.

Finally, remember that schools and church youth work often run similar recreational programmes. You could put a school in touch with facilities such as residential centres or entertainment venues, and many Christian centres run midweek programmes that may complement the work you are doing.

Visits

'I never knew churches had basketball courts!' That's how one nine-year-old responded to a visit with his school to a Baptist church. The church was celebrating its centenary and had arranged some special visits from local schools. Their youth worker and a Scripture Union schools worker, who was a member of the church, had devised an imaginative programme to ensure that the pupils saw the church as a living community and not just a century-old building.

One of them dressed in Victorian costume and took the pupils back in their imagination to the time when the church was established. The other then brought them into the present and gave a picture of what was going on in the church today, including a visit to the basketball court in the church hall! A demonstration of a baptism, the chance to meet some church members and some refreshments ensured that the pupils went away with the realisation that the church was much more than a building and something they could enjoy. A significant indicator of the success of the visits was the display of 'thank you' letters from the pupils that soon appeared in the church.

Many churches are involved in similar links with schools because RE teachers are often keen to take pupils to visit places of worship. A church that makes the extra effort to ensure such a visit is imaginatively presented and pitched at an appropriate level for the pupils will usually be well received by the school.

Visits are a relatively simple way in which churches and schools can work together constructively, and not only in RE. A unit of work on Victorian Britain (or another relevant historical period) can be brought to life by the imaginative use of a church building. One church actually arranged a demonstration wedding as part of some work on marriage. And, of course, it would not be too difficult to work co-operatively with a local undertaker and help pupils to discover what happens at a funeral!

Some churches produce a funsheet with things for pupils to discover through exploring the building. Many cathedrals have excellent educational programmes that take full advantage of the building as a historical resource whilst developing pupils' understanding of the relevance of Christian faith. Wherever possible, it is good if someone from the church can talk to the pupils clearly and briefly about what their faith means to them.

In the end, the most important thing is to use this kind of opportunity well and imaginatively. At a time when the majority of young people never set foot in a church building, to help them to have a positive experience of visiting a church has to be a good thing.

SUMMARY

- Try to raise your church's awareness of schools.

- Starting a prayer group:
    advertise it widely
    tell the school what you are doing
    arrange a suitable pattern of meetings
    try not to become exclusive
    pray for specific things
    keep confidences
    persevere

- Praying in church:
    include schools in the intercessions
    mention news from schools in church bulletins
    pray for church members who are in schools

- Churches can offer people:
    teachers, pupils, parents and others who are already involved
    support for Christian governors
    classroom assistance, eg reading
    adults to assist with trips and camps
    specific counselling and support
    people with specialist expertise for the curriculum, eg those from different professional backgrounds
    practical help around the school

- Churches can offer resources:
    use of church building
    books
    ideas and resources for RE

6

HELPING CHRISTIANS IN SCHOOL

If there is a front line (or maybe a chalk face!) in schools work, who is on it? I believe that it is the Christians who live and work in schools every day – not just pupils and teachers, but secretaries, meals' staff, technicians and others – people who are in school day in and day out, living out the gospel and speaking for Christ. Their witness should form the backdrop to any other kind of work in schools, and they deserve as much support as we can give them.

In a school Christian group I visited, one girl in particular was asking lots of questions. She talked about the fact that she had started to pray and read the Bible regularly. I could see the rest of the group were puzzled, and found out why afterwards when a teacher said that this girl had never been to the group before. She was one of the most troublesome pupils in the school. However, the teacher had noticed a difference in her recently. It turned out that the driver of the girl's school bus was a Christian. Over a period of months she had talked to him and discovered this. His witness led to her coming to Christ.

This is the essence of schools ministry but it is not what usually gets noticed. We are more accustomed to hearing about the work of organisations or schools workers. Yet this ongoing witness of Christians who are part of that community is at the heart of God's mission in schools. Unlike those of us who visit, these people don't get to walk away after they have done their bit. If a visitor to the school does something to upset people, these Christians are the ones who have to live with the consequences.

It is not too hard to imagine how the opportunities we currently have to work in schools might be lost. Changes in legislation could mean that collective worship disappears from the timetable. Similarly, RE might be reduced to an option or removed altogether – there are many countries around the world where it is virtually non-existent. A move to a continental day in which there was no lunch break would probably make voluntary groups impractical. And just as the climate towards visitors from outside has changed, making it possible for people such as schools workers to link up with schools, so it could move in the future in the opposite direction. The only area of schools ministry that is not to some extent vulnerable is that of Christians who are already part of the school community. It is nearly impossible to stop their witness.

Even in the harshest days of Communism in Eastern Europe, there were still Christians in schools. They may have been very restricted in what they could do and say, but they were there and could not be silenced. In Odessa in the Ukraine, Easter celebrations were replaced by a festival commemorating wartime liberation. One spring a teacher spent the whole week explaining the significance of this celebration of freedom. On (Maundy) Thursday she ended her final lesson about the occupation by saying to the class, 'So what will we be celebrating on Sunday?'

'Please, miss, the resurrection of Jesus Christ!' said a boy at the back of the class.

Part of the genius of Christian mission is that it does not depend on structures, methods or even opportunities. If Christians are there, so is mission. Yet so often the existing presence of Christians is the last thing we consider. I believe that the Christians who are already *in situ* have to be our starting point. They do not have to do everything, but they should be involved and considered in other people's thinking.

Therefore, an important part of ministry to schools is to support Christians in schools. This is not just because we want to help them survive in their faith where they are (although that is a worthy motive in itself!). It is because they have a crucial impact on anything else that takes place, and they are in the unique position of being able to make the most of opportunities that do not often come the way of those who are outside schools.

I once took a series of school assemblies and calculated that over a period of a few days I had spoken to more than 2,000 people. Whilst it was a great opportunity, I could also see the limitations. For one, I had only spoken to these people for about six minutes first thing in the morning when their concentration was probably on the low side. But even more important, those pupils and teachers knew nothing of my life; they had no idea whether it matched my words. As an outsider I could not do much more than speak.

On the other hand, there were quite a number of Christians in those schools. Every day they lived their lives in the open. The people around them could see whether Christ had really made a difference to them, what happened when they were under pressure and how they treated other people. They could see the commitment that these Christians had to each other. In other words, they were able to see the affect of the gospel. The lives of those Christians, hopefully, went hand in hand with the words I had spoken at school assemblies. Both were important. Our ministries were complementary.

Since the witness of Christians in schools is so significant, what can we do to support them?

Recognise their important role
Unfortunately, there is a problem that undermines the importance of the witness of 'ordinary' Christians in schools: this is that Christians are in danger of devaluing in general the ministry of people in the secular world. We are much more comfortable with what takes place in

churches and Christian organisations; it is easier to identify. Yet the fact is that a Christian pupil in a school is just as much called by God to serve as I am when I visit that school to speak in a Christian group meeting. Both of us are there as ambassadors of Christ. Unfortunately, people are more likely to pray for me than they are for that pupil, whose ministry may not even be acknowledged.

A teacher working in a mission school in Africa once told me that the two main differences between teaching in Africa and teaching in Birmingham were that the school in Africa was more rewarding because the pupils wanted to learn, and that her church now prayed for her because she was a missionary. Other than that, nothing had changed!

Christians in schools are not a special case. *All* Christians are called to serve, in their office, their street, their family or wherever they spend their time. This service is part of the ministry of the whole church. Because a church is not an institution but rather a body of God's people, its ministry does not just consist of the meetings on the church programme. Its ministry is the sum total of the ministry of the people who make up that body, whether it is organised by the church or not. Looked at in this way, we see it differently. For one thing, there is probably more going on than we realise, and we can rejoice in that. But we may also recognise that some of the 'outside' things people do are more significant than some of the 'inside' things, and this may change our priorities.

If we are really concerned about reaching young people with the gospel, it may be a better use of limited resources to support a teacher in her work with a school Christian group than to leave her running a struggling church youth group. In school she will probably have contact with many more young people than she ever will in church.

By encouraging young people in their involvement in school, we can help them to become strong in their witness. This doesn't just mean getting them to go to the Christian group. There are many other areas of school life where

Christians can be effective, not least in simply being a good friend. I knew some Christian pupils who deliberately did *not* go to the Christian group in their school because they wanted to witness to their friends and the group would have got in the way of them doing this. These pupils met together out of school to pray for their friends. In situations like this it really helps to know that other Christians acknowledge and value what you are doing. A conversation about school or a public mention in church can do wonders in helping someone realise that what they are doing is noticed and appreciated.

Understand their situation

David Livingstone, the nineteenth-century missionary explorer, returned to Britain to speak about his work and the problems he faced. 'It's hard being a Christian in Africa,' he said, 'and it's hard being a Christian in Britain.' It is certainly true that being a Christian is difficult anywhere, but this should not lead us to play down the enormous pressures there are on Christians in schools. One way in which we can encourage their ministry is to try to understand what it is like for them.

Christian pupils have to face the same issues of growing up as everyone else, but they also have the challenge of being distinctive because of their Christian faith. For adolescents it is more complicated still. They are developing their own identity, becoming increasingly independent of parents and family. Peer pressure can be particularly strong at this stage and, as they find their identity within a different group, their Christian faith may come under a lot of strain, especially if it is a faith they have inherited from their family rather than worked out for themselves.

It is not just teenagers who face pressure. In primary school, children are aware that being a Christian makes them different. What do you do when you go to a seven-year-old friend's birthday party and find that everyone is watching a horror video you would never see at home? How do you react when a friend wants you to lie to get them out of trouble? What do you do when your friends laugh at the Bible you were given for your birthday? These issues are not all new and some may become more acute later. Nevertheless, they are a significant part of life for many children.

Adults who work in schools may also be facing some of these issues, but there are others as well. The sheer pressure that teachers have faced over the past few years has taken its toll. Many have found that a job they once found satisfying has become a frustration. Instead of working with pupils much of their time is taken with administration and meetings. Teachers who in the past would have helped to run a school Christian group can no longer fit it in. They feel guilty about this and misunderstood by other Christians who don't realise why this has happened.

In common with many other areas of life, education has undergone great change in the past few years. The pace of this change has left many exhausted and unable to cope with any more. I know of a minister who felt his church needed to change but found that the congregation faced so much upheaval in other areas of their lives that more in church would have been the last straw.

There are more subtle pressures on teachers. As with pupils, the breakdown of Christian consensus means that people who hold Christian values are increasingly in the minority. There are a greater number of situations where Christians may feel out of step with the people around them. The values inherent in the curriculum are often a challenge. Some feel awkward about books that are being studied or productions that are being staged. Being different is certainly an authentic part of the Christian's experience, but it is no less difficult because of this.

The best way of gaining a better understanding of what Christians face in school – both pupils and those who are paid to be there – is simply to talk to them about it. When we come together as Christians, we need to give ourselves space to share the pressures facing us outside church and allow this to flow into intercession for each other. By so doing, we may do more for ministry in schools than we realise.

Provide them with resources

If you can't go into a school, you may be able to help the Christians there by providing resources. This help need not be financial – there are many other resources that you may have access to. Open homes are very valuable: a group of Christian teachers may need somewhere to meet that is convenient for school; a prayer group might want a base; some young people might simply want a friendly place where they can drop in with their friends after school. If you have access to a holiday home, it can be a great boon to a group who want to get away for a residential weekend.

Transport is a major issue for young people. Many adults take it for granted that they can get around easily, but children and teenagers are usually dependent upon other people transporting them. So willingness to drive a group of youngsters around will not just be a great help, it will also challenge them to ask why an adult should put themselves out for them in such a way.

Do you have equipment that you can lend? Tents, sports equipment, games and the like would all be useful for a group running a camp, so think what you have in your garage. Books and videos may sit on your shelf unused for most of the time, yet be invaluable to a group in school. In your place of work you may have access to waste materials and off-cuts. It is often the simple things that are useful, so be imaginative.

Someone who is good at design or artwork can be of real help. Posters, handouts and display materials are all useful to Christian teachers or groups. School groups, particularly in primary schools, often want to use music but may not have a musician. If you can play something, you may be able to contribute in this way, even if only on an occasional basis.

Do what they cannot do

Christian ministry is about partnership. Primarily, this means partnership with God because it is *his* ministry: we join in with it, we don't initiate it. However, it is also about partnership with other Christians, whether or not we are conscious of how our work comes together: 'I planted the seed, Apollos watered it, but God made it grow,' said Paul (1 Cor 3:6).

Work in schools likewise runs on partnership. Sometimes people outside a school will be supporting something which Christians inside are doing. At other times, a visitor will do something with the support of Christians in the school, ie a schools worker might lead assemblies knowing that Christians in the school have been praying for him. What we want to avoid is overlap and competition, so a good principle is to try to do what people in the school cannot.

One thing that Christians in school often lack is time. If you have spare time in the day, you certainly have something to offer. Some Christian groups are led by people from outside the school for just this reason. In one school the deputy head was a keen Christian but just too busy at lunchtime to commit himself to the school's Christian group. So, a mum from a local church, whose children used to be at the school, organised the group while the deputy head did the liaison within the school, announcing the group's meeting times on the PA, making sure there was a room available, and so on. You don't have to be a great leader or youth worker to help run a Christian group. Your role might simply be to arrive before everyone else rushes in, make sure that other people have planned what is happening, provide some drinks and generally oil the wheels.

Another thing that someone from outside can do is to bring perspective. If you go to the same school day after day, it is easy to get discouraged. As a schools worker, or someone in a local church with a concern for schools, you can bring people together so that they see something of the bigger picture.

There may be all kinds of expertise locked up in the local church. A friend of mine who is a vet used to visit schools with me. The pupils loved it because he had treated most of their pets. The strange thing was that when I asked how the pets were, they had almost always died! And a schools worker I know has made a point of finding out in her church who has an interesting job or story. She then links them up with Christian groups and teachers so that they can visit schools or speak. Most of them are people who would not have thought of themselves as the kind of person who could work in school. And most of them were unknown to the teachers and group leaders.

Pray

This section may be predictable but this does not lessen its importance. I mentioned earlier the missionary who said that it was only when she began working abroad that her church prayed for her, and her story is probably not unusual. Yet if Christians are on the front line of witness in schools, they need our prayer. One schools worker took photos of the Christian groups in the local schools. He then gave copies to local churches, encouraging them to display the photos on the missionary notice board as a reminder to pray. A prayer group I know invited the Christian teachers at a local primary school to lunch and a time of prayer. For the teachers, to know that people were supporting them in this way was a great encouragement.

There may be a teacher in your house group whom you could pray for regularly. Alternatively, why not adopt a Christian group at a school in your area and pray regularly for them, keeping in touch with all their news, and helping out where you can?

By now you may have begun to realise, if you did not before, that there is a lot of 'hidden' work going on in schools, often done very quietly by people who just get on with it as part of their normal routine. However, it is also true that all kinds of people who would never think of themselves as schools or children's or youth workers can play a significant role in supporting the unsung heroes in school. You might like to think through whether you have a contribution to make.

SUMMARY

- Acknowledge, as publicly as you can, the important role of Christians in schools.

- Try to understand their situation and the enormous pressure they are under.

- A Christian pupil will face:
    the need to be accepted
    the need to be distinctive as a Christian

- A Christian teacher will face:
    work pressures
    a rapid pace of change
    being in the minority

- Talk to people about their experiences in school.

- Provide resources to help in their ministry:
    open homes
    transport
    equipment
    skills, eg music, art

- Provide regular prayer support.

7

VOLUNTARY GROUPS

A twelve-year-old girl invited a new teacher to a meeting of the Christian group in her school. She had no idea whether the teacher was a Christian or not. Years later, the teacher told me what happened: 'As soon as I entered the room,' she said, 'I knew that God was there.' Unknown to the girl, much earlier, when the teacher was at university, she had prayed. She was not a Christian nor was she at all sure that God existed. Her prayer was that if God was real he would make himself known. Now, several years later, he had answered that prayer through a small group of Christian pupils in a school.

There are groups like this in schools all over the world, and no two are alike. Some are linked with larger organisations such as Scripture Union or Inter Varsity Fellowship. Others are quite independent, unknown to anyone outside their area. They exist in all kinds of schools – state and private, primary and secondary. Some are led by teachers, some by pupils and some by people from outside the school.

Two factors link these groups: the first is they exist because someone has a vision for serving God, and the second is that they are voluntary. This means that they offer young people different ways of learning. According to Brian Hill, this principle of voluntary learning is 'the best-kept secret in education theory' (*Catalyst 4*, Scripture Union International). Informal settings such as Christian groups are very effective, for the simple reason that people are there because they *want* to be there. This is an important

difference between Christian groups and religious education. Even in Christian schools, teachers will often see the
value of running a voluntary group alongside RE.

No special privileges

Because voluntary groups are not part of the official school
curriculum, they are quite legitimate in a secular school.
They are not seen to represent the official stance. Where
many religions are represented amongst the pupils, voluntary groups can exist without the school appearing to
favour one religion over another. Christians are not asking
for special privileges. In some schools there is, for example,
a Jewish group as well as a Christian one. Even where a
Christian group is the only one in existence, the fact that it is
voluntary can override the apparent problems of pluralism.

In one school in a very ethnically and religiously diverse
surburb of Melbourne, Australia, there was a small but
lively Christian group. One of the teachers complained to
the school council about the existence of this group. His
argument was that, whilst there were students of several
different religions represented within the school, the only
religious group to meet was the Christian one – and this
constituted favouritism. The school council investigated
and discovered that this was just about the only voluntary
activity in the school that was working. So, rather than do
away with it, the council affirmed the group's existence and
encouraged others to start similar ones! The key issues to
their decision were that the group was voluntary and the
opportunity to run a group was open to anyone who would
accept the school's way of working. This gave the school a
safeguard when it came to people who might abuse the
privilege of meeting in school, apply unfair pressure to
pupils, and so on.

Different shapes and sizes

School Christian groups come in all shapes and sizes. Some
are made up mainly of Christians; others most definitely are

not. I am amused when I sometimes hear people apologise because there are so few Christians in their group! The important thing is not so much who is in the group as what the group is about. Whether it is made up of Christians, people who have yet to come to know Christ, or a mixture of the two, what matters is that the group bears witness to the good news of Jesus.

Traditionally, for many people the starting point has been a group of Christians wanting to meet together to serve Christ. This opens up exciting potential for developing young people with confidence in the gospel and a radical concern to change the world. The stakes are high because school is not necessarily a comfortable place for Christians, and it is easy to opt out and go underground. On the other hand, if a person learns to trust Christ in the school context they will be ready to live for him wherever they find themselves in the future.

One school group has written their own manifesto, which makes a great model for radical discipleship:

'What we stand for/against'

● This group wants to be a witness, to [the school's name] and beyond, of the truth of God and the values of heaven.

● We want to be good news in the school: to spread respect for God, other people, the school and ourselves. We want to offer friendship to everyone in [the school's name], because we believe we are all equal before God. We want to help make [the school's name] a better, happier school. We are eager to serve God by helping others in [the school's name], and by helping in practical ways at school events.

● We want to resist wrong in the school: to resist intolerance, bullying, violence (verbal and physical), racism, sexism, immorality, bad language, teaching opinions as facts (eg Darwin's theory of evolution), cynicism.

- At times people will accept this group; at other times people may laugh at us or worse. At all times we will do our best to serve God and those around us sincerely.

'What we want to do'

- We want to share with our friends our faith in God and one another. We will seek to do this not by trying to push our views on other people, but by living the Christian life, leading others by our example.

- We will continue to develop a social life out of school which is fun and healthy.

- We will continue to play a role in [other local school groups]. We will develop our friendships with Christians in those schools.

- We want to get the reputation of being the best group in the school, because of our friendliness, fun and faith. We want the group to grow in numbers and in understanding. We want a variety of activities – Bible teaching and prayer, discussions, football games, special guest meetings where we introduce friends to the group.

- We want to run another weekend house party.

- We want to lead assemblies from time to time.

- *We want to be good news in our school and our families, using our lives for something good which will last for ever.*

School groups are not always built around a core of Christians. Some are more like evangelistic clubs, and their programme makes no assumptions about the Christian background or knowledge of the people who come. The aim is to introduce people to Christ and provide them with the opportunity to grow in their relationship with him.

Their format means that these groups are often more in touch with younger pupils, and they can be found in both primary and secondary schools. Having said this, there are plenty of exceptions, and many groups involve older pupils. Sometimes a school will have two, one for Christian pupils and another, perhaps run by those pupils, which is more like an evangelistic club.

Both of the kinds of groups I have described appear to be quite formal, whatever their style in practice. They have programmes and meetings and take quite a lot of organisation and planning. This is not the only way, however. In some schools there are groups that are much more informal, so much so that they can hardly be called groups. In reality, these groups are simply friends who get together.

One teacher I know would spend most of her lunch-times in her classroom, marking and preparing for the afternoon. Some of the pupils in her class would come in occasionally to help, and out of this grew a different kind of Christian group. They never had formal meetings, but many of their conversations were about Christian things. Sometimes the teacher would suggest an idea: making and selling biscuits for a Christian charity and cleaning up a part of the school are just a couple of the things they did. The key factor was not the activity, but the relationships between them. Out of these relationships came real interest and growth in the Christian faith.

For the teacher, running this group almost came as second-nature. I'm not sure she really was aware that she was running a group – she liked the pupils and this was a way to get to know them better! Her Christian faith came out as a natural part of her life, and the pupils, many of whom had never come across Christians in any direct way, saw faith at work in a real person.

God's people in school
In the New Testament the Christian community of God was fundamental to evangelism. Jesus said to his disciples that

they must love one another because 'by this all men will know that you are my disciples' (John 13:35). Real Christian fellowship is inevitably evangelistic. It seems clear from Acts 2:42–47 that the community life of the early Christians had an evangelistic impact: 'All the believers were together and had everything in common . . . Every day they continued to meet in the Temple courts. They broke bread in their homes . . . praising God and enjoying the favour of all the people. And the Lord added to their number daily those who were being saved'. Likewise, in schools we must not take lightly the impact of Christian community in drawing people to Christ.

I was at a school for a lunch-time meeting. A teacher and a handful of pupils were there, and one of the pupils was leading the meeting. For twenty minutes they played silly games, whilst I got increasingly frustrated. When, I wondered, was the 'serious' part going to start?

All the way through the meeting the classroom door was partly open. I noticed a boy walk down the corridor a number of times. Each time, he stopped at the door and looked in. Eventually, he put his head around the door, asked if he could come in, and then joined in with the games.

Afterwards I talked with the teacher. She explained that their main meeting, a prayer meeting, was on a different day and this was simply the Christians getting together for fun. As for the boy who had come in part way through, she was amazed that he had come along. He was in a lot of trouble, seemed to have no friends and was about to be thrown out of the school because of his behaviour.

I hope I learnt my lesson! Apart from teaching me not to be so hasty in jumping to conclusions, this was a simple but profound example of the importance of Christian community. The fact that they didn't do anything 'serious' was quite irrelevant. That boy found a place in this group, even if only for a brief time, which he could find nowhere else in school. That little meeting of Christians had become one more demonstration of the power of the gospel to break down barriers.

Bible reading

In many parts of the world, school Christian groups are synonymous with Scripture Union. The emphasis on encouraging people to read the Bible daily, systematically and obediently, together with Scripture Union's provision of relevant Bible reading resources, has often been the backbone of a Christian group. At the heart of this approach to reading the Bible is the belief that God longs to speak to us through his word, if only we will give him the opportunity. Christians whose lives are being transformed as they live out the scriptures are surely going to make an impact on people around them. I am convinced that one of the vital functions of a school group is to help people get the habit of reading the Bible regularly.

This approach is not just for those who have been Christians for many years. When I was teaching, I met weekly with three pupils who had made a commitment to Christ during a mission – I was trying to help them get into reading the Bible. We would simply spend thirty minutes together after school, reading that day's Bible passage, together with the comments in a Scripture Union Bible guide. Then we would talk about anything that had come up during the previous week's readings and pray together. It was a simple way of helping those young people, who were totally new to the Bible, to begin the disciplines of the Christian life.

Into action

School Christian groups present a great opportunity, but how do you get a group started? Obviously, this chapter cannot cover everything, and there is other literature to help, such as that from Scripture Union (see the list at the end of this book). However, let's look at some of the principles that will help you to get going.

Making contact

Use the principles outlined in chapter three for contacting the head teacher and doing the preparation needed beforehand, so that you can make a good case for starting a group in the school. Remember – don't be a Lone Ranger. Even if other Christians in the school cannot do much, it's good to have their support and prayer (see chapter six). A Christian leader or pupil in a school may already know other people who would be interested in taking part. In a primary school it may be a matter of speaking to Christian parents you know. Nevertheless, there are likely to be sympathetic people whom you don't know, so do your best to find them. Announcements in school, in assembly and in bulletins, are one way to find people who might be interested. More may turn up than you expect! One teacher announced in assembly that she was starting a Christian group. Later that day, two girls came to her rather sheepishly and told her that there had been a group there for two years already. I suspect that the fact she didn't know about the group indicated how much it needed her help!

School communications are not infallible, so contact local churches and youth groups as well. Not only will this put you in touch with people you might have missed, it may help you get support from within the churches. Someone reluctant to come along may do so with a bit of encouragement from their church. If nothing else, the churches will be made aware of what is going on.

All this might seem a bit slow if you are eager, but good preparation pays off in the end.

First thoughts

When you have identified those who are interested, get together to talk about your ideas. Try not to be too fixed in these to start with. Together you may come up with something much better than you imagined. Prayer is obviously an important part of the process and another reason for not rushing things along.

Whether it is a primary or secondary school, and whether you are from inside or outside it, there are some basic questions and issues to work through:

Why do we want to do this?
What are we trying to achieve?
Who is the group aimed at?
Where will it meet?
When will it meet?
What will we call it?
Who will take overall responsibility for running it?
Who will do what?
What are we going to do next?

Here are some things to take into account as you discuss those issues.

• Leadership
Primary school groups are, not surprisingly, led by adults. Whilst these are often teachers, they may just as easily be parents or volunteers from outside school. The important factor is that there is a good working relationship between whoever is leading and the school. It may be that whilst a teacher is too busy to lead a group regularly, he can be the link that ensures everything runs smoothly for a leader from outside.

Even though this is very adult-oriented, it is worth remembering that there are many ways in which children can help, even though they are not taking responsibility. There is no better way to develop their commitment to a group than for them to have a part in making it happen. Try to avoid spoonfeeding them!

In secondary school groups, things tend to be a little different. There was a time when most groups were led by older pupils, with encouragement from behind the scenes by teachers. Today, for a variety of reasons, teachers and other adults tend to take a more direct role in leadership. It is not at all uncommon for a group to be led by, say, a youth worker from outside the school. There is a danger, however, that the group becomes yet one more thing which is done to or for young people. So much youth work is of good quality, yet disables young people themselves from being able to organise and lead.

There are plenty of horror stories of groups led by pupils that were an absolute disaster, either because their enthusiasm got them into trouble, or because the whole thing was incredibly dull and boring. But then the same is true of some groups run by adults! When pupils are involved in running groups well, they have a number of advantages over adults.

For one thing, they generally do not have to adapt to the culture of the pupils – they are already part of it. Not only that, pupils can all too easily dismiss what adults say – however much those adults are in touch – on the grounds that they don't understand because they are of another generation. This argument loses much of its weight when it is other pupils they are speaking about! There is a real sense in which young people can be the most effective in reaching their peers.

Another crucial reason for involving pupils in leadership is that training others is a central aspect of Christian ministry. According to Paul, one of the key functions of apostles, prophets, pastors, evangelists and teachers is 'to prepare God's people for works of service' (Eph 4:12). School can be a superb training ground for young Christians, but it usually means extra effort on the part of others.

So, if you are an adult, even if you are a teacher, don't assume that you have all the answers. Pupils themselves have a great deal to contribute and to gain from taking on leadership. On the other hand, if you are a pupil, don't forget that teachers and youth workers could be a great help to you. Their experience may far outweigh any problems you may see. In fact when young people and adults are seen to be working together, it is one more demonstration of the power of the gospel to break down human barriers: 'for you are all one in Christ Jesus' (Gal 3:28).

● Aims

If you do not know what you are trying to achieve, you will probably not achieve it! Start by identifying the target membership of the group. Are you aiming at one particular age range or everyone in the school? Is the group chiefly for Christians, non-Christians or a mixture of the two? What the group does will largely be determined by who is in it.

There is a lot to be said for not making too great a distinction between an evangelistic group and one for Christians. People who are new to the gospel need to approach it in ways that are relevant and that don't assume they know anything. But Christians benefit from this too as they are shown ways to communicate the gospel to their friends. On the other hand, the dimensions of Christian discipleship that a group for Christians might address are important, and people need to be aware of these before committing themselves to Christ. Counting the cost of following Jesus can only mean something if a person has some understanding of what discipleship means.

Thus your aims will probably relate to those for whom the group exists and what the group is setting out to achieve. A good overall aim is for everyone involved to move closer to Christ. For some this will simply mean that they start to think about the Christian faith; some will make a significant commitment to Jesus himself; and some will continue to grow in obedience to him. Out of this other aims may arise, such as studying the Bible, prayer, fellowship, and so on.

● Age range

Groups rarely work well where the age range is too wide, because pupils' interests vary so much. So, whether the group is in a primary school or a secondary school, think hard about whom the activities will be pitched at. In some schools the problem is solved by having more than one group. However, if there are multiple groups within the school, it will be necessary to create the sense of them all belonging together. One way to achieve this is by having occasional joint meetings, possibly out of school, for example a residential weekend or camp.

● Place

All too often Christian groups 'hide' themselves away. Seclusion may accommodate a desire for peace and privacy, but it also gives the impression that the group is sealed off from the outside world. What makes a good location for a group is that it is easy to find, gives the group a decent profile and is comfortable. Science labs are not a good idea on the whole – sinks and gas taps tend to get in the way! I heard of a group in Jamaica that met under a tree. It was certainly public and the shade was very welcome, but I don't think it would be very practical in Britain. On the other hand, who knows?

Sometimes the school building is not the best, or even a possible, meeting place. Some groups in France, for example, meet in community centres or churches because they are not allowed to use school premises. Sometimes, a nearby home may be good, but the problem with using one as a regular base is that it again separates the group from the school.

● Time

Most groups meet during lunch. In many schools this is a practical necessity because pupils leave immediately at the end of the day. On the other hand, the lunch break in most schools is very short, giving little time for any significant activity during the meeting. One way around this is to supplement lunch-time meetings with occasional gatherings after school, in evenings or at weekends.

Some schools are losing a common lunch break altogether as they switch to staggered lunch-times. This means, unfortunately, that there is no time when everyone is free.

Again, after-school meetings may be a possibility, or much smaller gatherings based on year-groups, supplemented by meetings out of school.

• Name
Depending upon which part of the world you live in, one name might be frequently used for school groups: ISCF (Inter School Christian Fellowship), Scripture Union and Christian Union are amongst the most common. Of course, within the school the name conveys a message about the group. Whilst one of the well-known names might help someone outside the school recognise the group, it might not have the same effect inside. It is worth trying to come up with a name that conjures up the image you think appropriate. The name you choose might also be a subtle indicator of whom the group is aimed at. Primary pupils and sophisticated sixth-formers will respond to rather different names.

Some groups go for something that is intriguing or even corny (one called itself 'BOGLE' – 'Because Our God Loves Everyone'). Others choose names that sound friendly but have intriguing theological ideas behind them, such as 'Saltpot' (and endless variations on the theme). Ironically, some stick with the old faithful titles but get away with it because of the quality of life that exists within the group. Whatever you opt for, don't choose it without some thought. The process may help you become clearer on what the group is about.

Getting permission
Once you have worked out your basic ideas, it is a good time to see the head teacher if you haven't done so already. You will have done enough thinking to show that you know what you are about, but you won't be so far down the track that your plans cannot be changed. The head may know something that you don't, which may affect them!

Before you speak to the head, try to think of the things he

or she will need reassurances about so that you are prepared. Even though heads make the decisions about what takes place in their schools, they are responsible to the governors and to the parents who entrust their children to the school. The head will want to be sure that you know what you are doing.

A starting point could be the advantages that a Christian group or activity would bring to the school. Christian groups are enjoyable voluntary activities for pupils. They provide an opportunity for Christian and non-Christian pupils alike to grow in their understanding of the Christian faith and to develop positive values. At all times be careful not to imply criticism of the school. 'We don't think the RE is very good' is not the best way of approaching things! Always remember you are going with a request, not a demand. Schools have plenty to do without having to deal with awkward Christians.

Many head teachers will want to know what demand there is for this activity from the pupils. It always helps, particularly if you are from outside the school, if you can show that there are pupils and parents who are interested. Secondary school heads will very often give permission for a group if the request comes from pupils, whereas they may be quite cool to an approach from outside.

As you will be dealing with children and young people, the head will want to know that you are responsible and trustworthy. If you are from outside the school and relatively unknown, it is obviously harder for a head to make a judgement, so recommendations from respected people in the community could be important. He or she will be concerned that you do not put inappropriate pressure on the pupils and that you understand educational issues. For example, pupils in year 4 will need to be treated differently from those in year 10.

The issue of home and parents may arise at this point. Primary heads may insist on parents giving permission before pupils can attend. A simple letter and reply-slip sent home will usually be appropriate. Even though secondary heads may not insist on this, keeping parents informed about the group is a worthwhile thing to do. Some groups run an occasional parents' meeting, with food and an interesting programme. It can be a good way of avoiding unnecessary suspicion and misunderstanding.

Of course, this is not just a question of avoiding problems with parents. There is a much more positive dimension. Although it is easy to think of pupils in isolation, the fact is that they are part of a family. A young person's family life is something that God is concerned about, and we ignore this at our peril.

Another area where the head teacher may well want reassurance is that of church connections. Many heads are afraid that a group will be too closely linked with one particular local church or denomination. This can be particularly sensitive for church youth workers, and it really does help if they are seen to be working with Christians from different churches.

Related to this is the issue of other faiths. Don't be surprised if you are asked why *you* should be allowed to start a group when there are so many other faiths around. My response is that I have no objection to other people doing the same as long as we have to work on the same terms and are all required to treat the pupils responsibly. Remember that we are not asking for exclusive favours for Christians.

Having said that, not all heads will give you the third degree! Many will be delighted that there are people who want to start such a group and will give you as much help as they can. However, even where there is more reluctance, good arguments and a positive attitude will get you a long way.

Second thoughts
Hopefully, you will by now have permission from the head and be ready to go. Now you have to decide quite what you are going to do.

Planning is very important but does not come naturally to everyone! Too little and you have chaos, too much and the atmosphere is a bit mechanical. So try to ensure that your planning has a human face. Thinking out a programme for a term in advance will mean that you have a good idea of where the group is going. On the other hand, asking people what they think and checking out your plans as you go along will help you be responsive to the group's needs.

A good way to approach programme planning is to see it in two dimensions: content and method. Defining your content and themes helps to maintain a balance in the programme. Your aims are very important here. If these are not reflected in the themes, you probably need to rethink either your aims or the programme. However, methods are also very important. You can have great content yet never communicate it because everyone is asleep!

A useful framework for content might be Bible teaching, prayer, evangelism, fellowship and service. Remember, though, that these are not neat and tidy categories: evangelism might well happen through studying the Bible together. Not only that, the balance between the categories will depend very much on who is in the group and what is needed at a particular time. Nevertheless, having the framework in place can ensure that the group doesn't get lopsided.

The methods you use will depend on many factors: the age and background of the group, its gifts and abilities, the facilities available, time constraints. One thing worth taking into account is that different people learn in different ways. One person will love a story whilst someone else wants lots of lively games. Another person is into heavy intellectual arguments whilst someone else always prefers a video. Not only that, individuals respond to methods differently at different times. So, using a variety of approaches is very important.

The list of possible approaches is endless. And whilst the age of group members is a significant factor to take into account, don't assume that a particular approach can only be taken with one age group. Often it is the way in which something is done that is important. I have seen seventeen-year-old boys loving a story really intended for seven-year-olds simply because they were not being patronised and could enjoy it at their own level.

Here is a basic list of methods that can help you keep your programme varied. Of course, a list of this sort is just a start – it may spark off your imagination. You might find it helpful to combine several different methods in one event:

games	simulation exercises
discussion	speaker
Bible studies	video
debate	music
social events	art/craft
competitions	food
story	quiz
prayer	drama

There are many resources available that will help put flesh on your ideas or even inspire you in the first place (see p 141). Several of these resources are produced with church situations in mind, however, so you will need to watch things like the amount of time they need and the background knowledge they assume. Likewise, think carefully about the age, ability and interests of the people in the group; some ideas don't seem quite so good when you look at them with these in mind.

Planning meetings is all very well but if no one turns up it is a waste of time. Publicity can be as imaginative as you like, but remember – the way you pass on information conveys a message often as powerful as the information itself. So whether it is a poster on the noticeboard, an announcement in tutor groups, a notice in assembly or a publicity stunt in the yard, try to do it in a way that communicates something positive. Energy life, imagination and humour are all important qualities.

Finally, what happens when someone comes along expecting the group to match the hype and it doesn't? No matter how good our programme is, if someone feels excluded or embarrassed, this is the memory of the group they will take away with them. The opposite is also true: if Christ's love is seen in action, it will be remembered for far longer than the intricate programme that took hours to plan.

Unfortunately, the pace of school life can make it difficult to spend the time necessary to build strong relationships. This is why it is so useful for groups to spend time with each other out of school if at all possible. Meeting in homes, going out together, and so on, are all useful. Most effective, perhaps, is for groups to go away together. Even a 24–hour trip staying in a church hall can enable friendships to develop in a way that they never will if meeting is restricted to twenty minutes in a school classroom. Longer residential breaks, such as weekends and holidays, are tremendously effective in helping young people to see the gospel lived out; holiday activities like those run by Scripture Union are a great way to reinforce the work done in school.

Christian groups in schools are one of the great opportunities open to us. They happen away from our own turf, on relatively neutral ground; they can bring the gospel into a young person's everyday context and show how Jesus is still relevant to life today; and they provide the opportunity for a new generation of Christians to learn how to serve Christ 'in the market-place' where they live and work. Christian groups in schools deserve our best shot.

SUMMARY

- Before you start a group, make contact:
    with other Christians in school
    with the local churches

- Ask the right questions:
    why do we want to do this?
    what are we trying to achieve?
    who is the group for?
    where will it meet?
    when will it meet?
    what will we call it?
    who will take overall responsibility for running it?
    who will do what?
    what are we going to next?

- When getting permission from school to form a group:
    be well prepared
    have good reasons
    show that there is a need and demand
    be aware that children live in families

- The vital issues in forming a group are:
    developing relationships
    planning
    the content and activities of the group
    publicity

8

IN THE CLASSROOM

If the curriculum is central to the purpose of schools, it is not surprising that Christians should want to be involved in some way or other. As we have seen already, it is vital for Christian ideas to be out there in the market-place.

Clearly, Christian ideas are communicated every day through Christian teachers and not just in RE classes. Christians are commanded to 'be transformed by the renewing of your mind' (Rom 12:2) and, as this happens, the renewal should spill out into the world through our thoughts and ideas. Whatever subject a Christian is teaching, there is potential for it to be taught distinctively. This is not a question of indoctrination. No teacher is neutral: what they teach will always be influenced by their own values, assumptions and prejudices. Ironically, Christians are often more aware of their assumptions and therefore less likely to indoctrinate. The most dangerous teachers are the ones who do not even realise they have biases!

Those of us who are not teachers need to be aware of the significant contribution Christian teachers can make. One friend of mine tells of a former pupil who, years later, told her that she had become a Christian whilst at university. What made her open to the gospel was reflecting on the way in which my friend had taught her history, and connecting this with the fact she was a Christian.

Christian teachers who find their resources are limited can call on organisations like the Association of Christian Teachers which offer support by producing relevant resources and sponsoring courses and research in different curriculum areas.

Outside in

Christians from outside school have a contribution to make, perhaps as a 'visiting expert'. A Christian may be invited to a RE class so that pupils can hear what faith really means to a believer. Sometimes a teacher may ask a schools or youth worker to take a whole lesson or even series of lessons if they have the appropriate skills and can make a worthwhile contribution. There are also many moral issues on which Christians can offer a valuable point of view. Someone who comes from a committed standpoint can bring a perspective to a discussion that would be inappropriate from a teacher.

Christians with particular expertise may be invited to take part in specific curriculum topics. Sometimes there will be no obvious Christian connection, but often there will. Medical people may be called upon to make a contribution to sex education or other moral issues; local politicians could speak about their life in politics; older people or ex-servicemen could give an 'I was there' talk in a history lesson. In all these situations there could well be natural opportunities for Christians to talk about the relevance of their faith.

Taking lessons – the pros and cons

Schools or children's workers are often invited to take part in lessons in school. Whilst this can be a great opportunity there are drawbacks too, and it is important to face up to these.

On the positive side, taking part in lessons puts the Christian message on the agenda in the classroom. It may be there already, through the curriculum and through Christian teachers, but this kind of visit may reinforce it. Importantly, it gives pupils the opportunity to hear about faith 'from the horse's mouth', not just in an academic way.

Classroom work provides the opportunity to meet pupils who would never come to a Christian meeting. By giving them a (hopefully!) positive experience of meeting a Christian, some stereotyping of Christians can be removed. Simply helping a hard-pressed teacher can be of value in itself.

On the other hand, the classroom is a place of education, not preaching; you will have to adapt to a different style and accept some restrictions. This is not an easy adjustment for many people. A more subtle problem is to do with role. However you see yourself, as far as many pupils are concerned when you are in the classroom you are a teacher. For some youth workers in particular this can be a real problem. Similarly, some people are sensitive about the way in which education can institutionalise Christianity, concealing its life and vibrancy. Christianity is not just a set of ideas to be talked about in a classroom; it is about a relationship with the living God.

A more difficult issue, however, is the occasional problem of the teacher who uses visitors as an easy way out of teaching. It is always tempting to take an opportunity just because it is there, even though in the long run it might not be good for you or the teacher. There are a number of warning signs to look out for. One is when a teacher says you can teach anything you like rather than asking you to connect it with something on the syllabus. Another is when a teacher leaves you in the classroom and disappears for the rest of the lesson.

Both of these things create a number of problems. First, there is a legal problem. The teacher is responsible for the pupils in his or her care, and it is taking a risk, to say the least, to leave the class solely in your charge. For you, there is the problem of discipline. No matter how good your skills, you are in a difficult situation as an outsider. A situation may arise that you cannot handle. Equally, you are open to accusations of behaviour that it might be difficult to defend. This may sound a little alarmist, but we need to be particularly careful in the current legal climate. Teachers at least have a union to defend them!

Educationally, there are problems too. If the teacher doesn't know what you have done, how can he or she link it with the ongoing work of the class? Your contribution may be seen by the pupils as just filling time and not as important as the real work. If, on the other hand, the teacher is present, your lesson may gain credibility as pupils make connections with other things they have studied.

As with any opportunity at school, the important thing is to know exactly why you are taking it. You may agree to participate in a particular lesson on one occasion in one school because, although it has no direct Christian relevance, it will help to build a relationship with that school. On the other hand, you may turn down involvement in a RE class in another school because you know that it is well served by Christians and there are other worthwhile things that can be done elsewhere. Strategy is always a great help when it comes to making tricky decisions.

What now?

Let's suppose that you have been invited by a teacher either to take a lesson with one of her classes or to take part in a lesson she is teaching. The teacher will be there, you have a specific topic and she has explained why she has invited you. What do you do now? Obviously it will be a little easier if you are simply joining in one of her lessons, but the principles are the same.

In many ways, preparing for the classroom whether in a primary or a secondary school is similar to any other preparation, but its importance is highlighted by the fact that you are entering an environment usually inhabited by a different kind of professional. If we are to enter this world from outside, we have to be ready to accept its ways of working.

The planning chart on page 115 gives a survey of the issues to consider. The first group of items are factual and can be found out by asking the teacher. Start and end times are crucial. Schools run to a strict timetable and overrunning will win you no friends. Finding out about the venue is not simply a question of knowing which classroom to go to. There is all the difference in the world between teaching in a modern classroom, a large assembly hall and a science lab, and any of them are possible! The nature of the classroom may determine what you decide to do. If it is open plan you will inevitably be aware of other classes and will need to be particularly careful about things such as noise levels. Likewise, the age and background of pupils will have a crucial impact on how you plan the lesson. Asking what the pupils would be doing if you weren't there may seem a bit excessive, but believe me it can make a difference. The most difficult class I ever taught had missed their computer lesson because of my visit – unfortunately I only found out when it was too late! Checking on the facilities will at least save you from planning something only to find that it is not feasible because, say, it is impossible to use a video in that room or at that time.

Having done your basic research, the next step is to work on the lesson itself and to establish your aim. This may well have been set for you by the teacher ('We've been doing Easter. Could you do something on why you believe in the resurrection?') So your *aim* is something like 'To examine the evidence for the resurrection'. This is quite general, however, so you will need to be more specific and decide upon your *objectives* for that particular lesson. What these are will be determined not only by what you think is import-ant but also by the time available and the age of the pupils. You cannot do everything in one lesson, so try to keep it simple. One good idea communicated well is better than ten confused ones.

The next job is to decide upon your method. You could simply stand in front of the class and tell them all you know about the topic. Unfortunately, the pupils are not likely to learn a great deal unless you have unusual powers of communication! Three basic principles will help you to choose the best method to use.

● Start with the experience of the pupils

It is difficult for people to make sense of new ideas unless they can relate them to what they already know. None of the pupils will have experienced resurrection, so the challenge is to find a connection between their experience and the topic! The question is, what is there that the pupils are already familiar with that will help them understand better the evidence for the resurrection? You could start with a detective or a courtroom (closer to the experience of some than others!) as a way of asking how we decide the truth of events in the past. A different approach would be to give them an unlikely experience (!) by eating a daffodil in front of them, then asking how they would convince their parents that something so unlikely happened at school? 'I know it sounds crazy, but I saw it myself!' (This is a tried and tested idea, but make sure that you don't eat the green bits!) The age of the pupils will be one major factor in your decision as to which approach to take. Once you have made a connection with their own experience, you can help them to think about how we could check out something like the resurrection.

● Involvement assists learning

Have you noticed how much more quickly you learn to find your way around somewhere new when you walk or drive yourself rather than be driven by someone else. This is simply because *you* are involved. It is the same in the classroom. Passive techniques (eg listening) have their place but need to be complemented by activity. This can be in the form of discussion, reading, written activities, drama, and so on. The important thing is the involvement. Again, plan to do something that is appropriate to the pupils' age and skills.

• Feedback is crucial

Allowing an opportunity for feedback gives pupils a chance to clarify what they don't understand and to challenge the things with which they disagree. But feedback is also important for the teacher – it enables you to find out whether you really have communicated what you want to communicate. I remember my dismay as a RE teacher, when one pupil wrote in an exam that one of the ten commandments was 'Thou shalt not admit adultery'. At least I knew where I had failed and had the chance to explain the commandments again!

In the context of this particular lesson, you can get feedback in a number of ways. The obvious one is through class discussion, question and answer, but you may also try a written activity (worksheets as we used to call them) or a small group activity such as role play or discussion.

By now you will have a number of activities that you want to include. The test comes when you try to fit them into the time available. The 'Outline of lesson' section of 'Preparing a lesson' (on p 115) enables you to put your activities into some order and to find out whether you have sufficient time. You will need to take account of the fact that you will inevitably lose a few minutes at the start or finish of the lesson, so build in some flexibility. There is nothing worse than losing the key point of your lesson because the bell has gone! So be prepared to cut some material out if it looks as though you will overrun. However, whatever you do, remember the principles and don't cut corners. Finally, check what materials and equipment you will need (a daffodil in October?) and avoid the temptation to fill in the evaluation section before actually doing the lesson!

You have now reached the stage when it would be worth discussing your lesson with the teacher. Even though you may feel confident, it won't do any harm to get someone else's advice, and it will strengthen the sense of partnership between the two of you.

Obviously, there is much more detail to consider that we have not discussed. You will want to think through exactly how you are going to present your material. Looking at the evidence from the Bible would be a very useful exercise, but how will you do it? Will you give out Bibles or photocopied extracts? Which version and extracts will you use? Will you use any visual aids, eg diagrams, overhead transparencies? If so, do you need to take equipment? Your own story is important here: the teacher asked *you* to explain why *you* believe in the resurrection. How will you deal with this? What about the difficult questions – have you thought through the common objections? If you go in unprepared, you have only yourself to blame.

Delivering a lesson

Well, the big day has come, you are thoroughly prepared and all that remains is to get on with the lesson. You arrive at school in plenty of time, meet the teacher and are taken to the classroom. A few minutes later, at the end of break, the pupils come in, your heart rate increases and the moment of truth arrives.

There are two vital tasks facing you in the first few minutes. One is to get a grip so that you feel you know what you are doing. The other is to build a relationship with the class. If you don't do both, then your task will be much harder. Fortunately, the two can be combined. So before arriving, work out a little script in your head so that you can introduce yourself to the class. Pupils like to know about their teachers, so the more they know about you the better the relationship. It is important wherever you can to take your cues from the teacher. You need to strike a balance between your own informality and the style of the school.

On the way

As the lesson progresses, there are a number of key tasks for you as the teacher. One is to keep an eye on the time. Certainly you can let an activity run on if it is going well, but remember there is always a price to pay: something else will have to go.

Another monitoring task is to check on how well an activity is working. If you have given pupils a task to do in groups, go around and check that they are doing it. They may have misunderstood your instructions and need further explanation. Or they may have decided to talk about last night's football and need encouragement in a different direction! Never be afraid to change tack if a part of your lesson is not working. Teaching is a dynamic activity, not a static performance. If it was, you could simply put the lesson on video and stand back and watch.

Answering questions

'How on earth can you believe that rubbish about the Bible?' This was a question I was asked towards the end of a lesson in a school I was visiting. If nothing else, it was honest! Being ready to field this sort of question has to be a part of your armoury if you are going to be involved in the classroom. Questioning is an important activity throughout the lesson, because of the issue of feedback that we looked at earlier. However, open question times, particularly at the end of a lesson, are a useful opportunity to allow pupils to set the agenda. They can ask the questions that matter to them.

You may simply ask if there are any questions and be faced with a forest of hands in the air. On the other hand, and particularly with older pupils, you may be greeted by a deathly hush. After all, who wants to be shown up in front of everyone in the class? Pupils aren't stupid! One way round this is to give out slips of paper and ask people to work in pairs or small groups, thinking of the questions they would like to ask. They can write them down on the paper and hand it in to you. This has a couple of advantages. One is that pupils have a chance to check with others that theirs isn't a stupid question. Another is that the question is asked anonymously. Of course, if you make a feature of anonymity, you have to stick to it and not put people on the spot by asking if you've just answered their question!

Interestingly, the Bible deals with the issue of answering questions in the context of facing opposition. Peter's advice is straightforward: 'Always be prepared to give an answer to everyone who asks you to give the reason for the hope that you have. But do this with gentleness and respect . . .' (1 Peter 3:15,16). I have no doubt that the last thing in Peter's mind when he wrote this was a schools worker facing a group of pupils in a classroom, but it is relevant nevertheless!

Be prepared to give a reason

If you haven't done your homework – and I don't mean the night before – it will quickly show when you are on the spot. This doesn't mean that you have to be a professor of apologetics, but it does mean that you will need to have done some thinking.

Part of your preparation should be to consider the kind of questions you might be asked. These may be on:

- the existence of God
- what happens when we die
- why God allows suffering
- whether all religions are the same

Moral issues may crop up as well: euthanasia, abortion, animal rights and so on. One thing is certain – pupils will want to know what *you* believe and why.

There is nothing worse than the prepared answer – it usually sounds false – so it is not a matter of learning answers off pat. However, you can work out the bare bones of some responses. That way you will have an idea of the kinds of things you could say. A good exercise is to work with a friend, questioning each other as if you were in a classroom. You can be sure that when it is for real the questions won't come up in quite the same form, but you will feel a bit more confident.

Books on objections to the Christian faith (apologetics) are useful here, but you need to be careful. Things change quickly and the questions asked today are not the same as those of a few years ago, though, not surprisingly, the same issues crop up regularly in the media as they are fundamental human concerns. Keeping in touch with TV and newspapers will mean that not only are you more prepared in yourself, you will have a better idea of how other people are thinking and the ideas that are influencing them.

When you are the one being put on the spot, it is all too easy to feel as if you are in a 'Christian *v* lions' situation, with the Christian (ie you) trying desperately to avoid certain death. However, the reality is quite different. For one thing, if you have done your homework the likelihood is that you have thought things out more thoroughly than the person asking the question. And it is good to remember that Christians are not the only ones who have to face up to difficult questions – everyone does! So try not to be on the defensive all the time. You may achieve far more in the long run by leaving people with questions about their own point of view than by convincing them that you can justify your Christian belief. Henry Ford said, 'Thinking is the hardest thing there is. That's why so few people engage in it.' If you can get pupils thinking long after you have gone, you will have done them a great service.

Make it personal

Peter's advice was to give a reason 'for the hope that you have' and this is a crucial dimension of our work with young people. As Christians visiting school, we are not there to teach about ideas as though they were something abstract and 'out there'. Our task is to show pupils how the Christian faith is relevant to us and also to them.

To do this we have to try to get into other people's shoes and see things from their point of view. This involves trying to get in touch with what really concerns them and then addressing the gospel to their needs. When you are involved in discussion in a classroom, try to uncover the possible anxieties that lie behind a question. Often it will have been prompted by a particular situation, and it can help to ask the person why he or she has asked it. Someone asking a question that is related, say, to suffering may be going through a very painful time in his or her life. When pupils ask questions about suffering and death or about marriage relationships, these may be real situations for them or for others in the class, and we may be walking on eggshells. There is no place for a dogmatic and insensitive response. So, whilst an issue may be relevant to them, it may also be one about which they are very sensitive and you will need to take account of this.

Our own experience is also relevant. Try to think of the reasons and arguments that you have found convincing. Instead of giving an abstract answer, talk about what helped you to become convinced, assuming that you did, that is! For example, as a sixteen-year-old I remember seeing a courtroom drama that was about the evidence of the resurrection. It was the first time I had thought of it in those realistic terms. This experience helped me to realise that the evidence which convinced me can persuade other people too.

However, answering questions is not just an academic exercise. Truth should make a difference to the way we live. We need to be ready to explain why the things we believe matter to us. Being a Christian should make a difference; we need to be ready to explain how.

Be gentle, show respect
If what we have just said is true, and the truth does make a difference to how we live, the *way* in which we answer people's questions will be almost as important as the answers themselves. No wonder Peter told people to give their reasons for faith 'with gentleness and respect'.

We must keep in mind our overall purpose. We are not trying to score points or win an intellectual argument: we want to share Christ with people. This means we must be careful about the manner in which we respond. It is so easy to win the battle, yet lose the war. What have we really achieved if we win an argument and, in the process, confirm someone in their view that Christians are arrogant and bigoted?

One way in which we can ensure that our style is consistent with our message is by taking people's questions seriously. It is so easy to put someone down by treating their question as a bit silly. Yet, however obvious or ridiculous the question might seem to you, the fact it has been asked as a genuine question means that it deserves a serious response. Of course, some pupils will try to pull a fast one, but this will not be too difficult to spot. Even if they do succeed in making you look foolish, what does it matter? It is far better than you making someone else look stupid.

We show respect for a person by making sure that we at least try to answer his or her question. So take time to check that you really have understood what the question is really about. It is so easy to think that you know what it is and switch to a response you have stored away in your head, when actually what the person has asked was very different. Over-confidence can also lead to people saying things too strongly. I once heard someone tell a class that everything in the Bible had been proved to be true. This didn't convince anyone and just made the schools worker look silly, especially to the teacher!

Sooner or later someone will stump you with a question that you cannot answer. When this happens, there is only one thing to do and that is to admit your ignorance. It will usually win you more credit than if you bluff your way through. Admitting that you don't know often opens the way to raising the subject again later on. If you say, 'I'm sorry, I don't think I know. But I'll go away and try to find out and tell you what I think next time I see you', you not only show that you are vulnerable and approachable, you leave things open for future discussion.

Questions can be an extremely worthwhile part of a lesson, but don't judge their value purely by the liveliness of the discussion you had. If you have simply started people thinking, you have performed a great service. The greatest impact may have been on those who said nothing at all.

SUMMARY

- When preparing to visit a school, find out about:
  the exact timing
  where it will take place
  the age range of the pupils
  what would be happening if you were not there
  what equipment and facilities are available
  what the teacher would like you to do

- Plan your overall aim and specific objectives for the session.

- Choose your method:
  start with pupils' experience
  remember that involvement assists learning
  build in feedback from the pupils

- When taking a lesson:
  make sure that you are as prepared as you can be
  build a relationship with the class
  monitor the way in which the lesson is going
  keep a close watch on time
  be ready to answer questions appropriately
  don't let the lesson end in confusion

PREPARING A LESSON

Date .... Start time .... End time ....
Venue/classroom ....
....
No. of pupils .... Age and background of pupils ......
....
....
What would they usually be doing then? ....
....
....
Facilities available ....
....
....
Aim ....
....
....
Objectives ....
....
....
Method ....
....
....
Outline of lesson (include approximate timings) ....
....
....
Materials/equipment ....
....
....
Evaluation ....
....
....
....
....
....
....

9

SCHOOL WORSHIP

It was 8.45 on Tuesday morning. Six inches of snow had fallen overnight but we arrived at a secondary school in good time to take assembly. A grim-faced teacher met us at the door.

'You're from Scripture Union?' he asked. We admitted that we were and waited for the warm welcome to continue.

'You're evangelicals,' he told us, not pausing for us to agree. 'You don't believe in purgatory. I'm going to show you what it's like.'

At this, he took us to the entrance of the school hall. Inside, three or four hundred students of all ages were sitting around chatting. There seemed to be a worrying shortage of adults.

'It's chaos here this morning, sheer chaos,' he said. 'Only half the kids are here. Most of the staff seem to be stuck in the snow. Nobody knows what's happening, so we've put everyone into the hall. *You* take them.'

'How long have we got?' I said, trying to sound professional.

'I don't know,' he replied. 'You just start. I'll go and find out.'

True to his word, he left us to get on with it. As he disappeared out the door, the reality of the situation began to dawn. For the foreseeable future we were on our own. Simultaneously, four schools workers felt a call to work alongside crocodile-infested rivers in a hot country.

We were new to each other as a team (this was the first

day of a mission week) and so had a very limited repertoire. This made choosing easy. Although the programme we had prepared was not appropriate for all the students (what programme would be?) we decided to launch into it.

Given the circumstances, it went well – but there was still no sign of the teacher. We began to fear that he had got lost in a snowdrift down a remote corridor. When at last he did reappear, we were literally in the middle of our last idea. Never has a 'Two minutes left!' stage whisper been more welcome.

The events of that morning were not quite what Parliament had in mind when it passed the law requiring schools to provide daily, collective worship. The weather – with a little help from the teacher and ourselves – had turned the event into a farce. Yet, though it was unusual (at least for days without snow), it is a good reminder of the reality of working in schools. No matter how experienced and well prepared you are, in a school anything can and may happen. You need to be ready.

HELPING WITH A PROBLEM?
Even when a school does not require snow-cover, school worship is an area in which Christians from outside can be a real help. At present the law requires maintained (ie government-funded) schools to provide a daily act of collective worship for all pupils. Whilst this is often referred to as 'assembly', technically the two are not exactly the same. (It is possible to have an assembly that does not include worship.) Nevertheless, in this chapter when I refer to 'assembly' I am referring to the collective act of worship required by the Education Act.

In most cases an assembly should be 'broadly and mainly Christian'. Consequently, a head teacher is responsible for providing five acts of Christian worship each week, even more if there is no place in which the whole school can meet together. This is more services than some clergy! However, head teachers face another problem in fulfilling their legal responsibilities. With less of the population regarding themselves as Christians, fewer teachers are happy to lead worship. Consequently, the burden tends to fall on the same willing few. An offer of help from outside can be very welcome.

If quantity is an issue for schools when it comes to collective worship, so is quality. It certainly matters to the people who run schools. Which school wants its pupils to spend, say, fifteen minutes of each day enduring something that seems boring and irrelevant? And it should also matter to Christians. I know of one or two adults who became Christians through school assembly, but I know many more for whom it was a real turn-off. The last thing we want worship to do is to inoculate pupils against the Christian faith. ('We'll give them just enough to make sure that they don't get the real thing . . .') Instead we should aim to leave pupils with a positive impression of Christian people and the Christian faith. If we do that, we will have achieved something very worthwhile.

The fact that your offer to help may be eagerly welcomed does not, however, mean that you can do whatever you like! The head has legal responsibility for what takes place. And you will (hopefully) want the school to have you back! So let's look at what you can do to make your contribution to collective worship a positive experience for the pupils, the teachers and yourself!

CHECKING IT OUT

Whether the initial approach has been made by you or by the school, understanding the situation into which you are going is crucial. So take time to talk with the school about their expectations, and try to explain what you feel you can contribute. Each school is different, so don't assume anything and be prepared to be surprised. I once visited a school where a classroom could be converted into a chapel: the pattern of the floor tiles incorporated a cross, and behind the blackboard was an alcove containing an altar and candlesticks!

Here is a check-list of things to discuss:

- date and time of assembly
- when and where to arrive
- age of pupils
- number of pupils
- time available to you (notices and the like can take lots of time)
- exact location (what kind of room?)
- facilities (PA system, screen, overhead projector, video, etc)
- subject (up to you, or is there a theme?)
- pupils' expectations (what are they used to?)
- teachers' expectations (prayer? hymn? no prayer? no hymn?)
- anything they would prefer you not to do!
- dress (do they expect you to dress fairly formally, or doesn't it matter?)
- other people (is it all right for you to take others with you if it is appropriate to what you plan to do?)

Phone the school a day or two beforehand to check the details of your visit, especially the time and date. A friend of mine arrived at 8.30 for a 9.00 assembly and sat in his car until 8.55. When he went into the school, he found that the pupils had been sitting waiting for him since 8.45: the teacher had given him the wrong starting time!

Likewise, make sure that you know exactly where you are going and how to get there, especially if it is your first visit to the school. I once arrived at a school only to find that the school was on two sites, and I was at the wrong one. If your visit is first thing in the morning, don't get caught out by peak-hour traffic – check how long it will take you. If you arrive at a church fifteen minutes late, you might not have missed much. Do the same at a school and it will probably all be over. It is much better to arrive in plenty of time, especially if you have equipment to set up.

Being aware of your own attitudes is another important part of preparation. *Why* are you doing this? Why do you think it is worthwhile? What are your motives? What worries you? If you are going to the school with someone else, talk about these things together. The questions will also set an agenda for your prayer beforehand.

Take time to think through the differences between the school situation and the contexts you are familiar with, especially if you are new to working in schools. If you are more familiar with working in a church environment, remember that your audience will not, on the whole, be there by choice – assembly is one relatively small part of a much longer day for them. So, if finishing on time is important in your church (and it may not be!) it is probably even more so in a school. The difference is that people will be thinking about the next lesson rather than Sunday lunch!

If you are more familiar with youth work situations, the issues may be different. Schools are very structured places and often quite formal. The pupils will have certain expectations of assembly and these may be surprisingly conservative. At the same time, you are the person you are and there is no point trying to be someone else. Try to be yourself in a way that is appropriate to the situation. You won't win any Brownie points for trying to be different for the sake of it. However, if you are straightforward and honest, that will be recognised and appreciated.

Finally, be ready to be flexible – schools are complex and people have to adapt to new situations. Take the story at the beginning of this chapter. By the time we got to the school, everything had changed – it had snowed! We could have told the teacher that we were only prepared for ten minutes with the year 8 pupils, but the school now had a different need – the pupils had to be occupied and contained until reinforcements (ie the rest of the staff) arrived. By being flexible we were able to help the school with a problem and therefore strengthen our relationship with it. Not only that, we met more of the pupils than we would have done if it hadn't snowed!

WHAT SHALL I DO?

The hardest part for many people is deciding what to do. You will be facing anything up to several hundred pupils and teachers. In a primary school, or in an assembly of the whole school in a secondary, the age and ability range may be vast. Most of them perhaps will have very little other Christian contact. How can you make the most of the opportunity?

Some people take the 'now or never' approach. This assumes that you won't be back again and these people will never hear the gospel again. So, you tell them as much as you can and ask them to respond, maybe by giving an 'appeal'. There are two problems with this approach. First, it is usually a self-fulfilling prophecy – you don't get invited back. Second, it puts most of the emphasis on the passing on of the message and almost nothing on its hearing. Now the content is extremely important, but unless that content is really heard and understood, no communication has taken place. It is like broadcasting a TV programme to a country where no one has a TV set.

Let's take a different approach. First, think of the people you are speaking to. Some of them will be mentally asleep, some will be thinking about something else (lunch, TV, their latest boyfriend or girlfriend, the holidays, and so on) and some will be waiting to see what this visitor is like. If you are really going to communicate, one major task is to get their attention. After that, if you manage to communicate one clear idea to them, given the short time available, you are doing well. If you also leave behind the memory that it was a good experience, you really are flying. In comparison with the 'now or never' approach, it seems like a limited aim, but for effective communication I suspect that it is much more realistic. If you do it well, the chances are there will be a next time when you can add a little bit more to the picture.

What do you want to communicate? It may be something suggested by the time of year – Christmas, Easter, and so on. It may be a basic Christian idea, especially if you are going to be there on a number of occasions and can work up a series. There may be a current issue in the news on which you can give a Christian perspective. You may have come across a misunderstanding about Christians that you want to correct; there may be something in the curriculum at the time, which will suggest an idea; or perhaps, most common of all, something in your own recent experience that seems just the right thing. Whatever you decide to take as your theme, it has to be relevant to the age and experience of the pupils. A Christian view of romance may be just right for year 10 but a bit beyond most in the reception class. (Don't bank on it though!)

The way you present your theme is at least as important as what it is. Again, a good rule of thumb is to start within the experience and interest of your audience. Telling your pupils that you want them to think about the issue of *ego* is likely to produce instant shut-down. But if you begin with some pictures of famous people and the images they present, you may get a different response. You can then relate this to the biblical idea, 'Man looks at the outward appearance, but the Lord looks at the heart' (1 Sam 16:7). I remember seeing a brilliant assembly on the theme of 'magnanimity', a word which does not trip easily from the tongue of the average pupil. The leader started by talking about the wording on the label of a sauce bottle! I can't quite remember how the link was made, but it certainly got everyone's attention very effectively.

Of course, there is more than one way to skin a cat, and there is more than one way to engage an audience with the theme. Here is a simple list for starters:

- visuals (overhead projector acetates, large sheets of card, etc)
- drama
- puppets
- stories
- audio-visuals (videos can be tricky in a large hall; filmstrips are so old-fashioned that they now have novelty value and will work in a large room)
- songs
- games
- audience participation

Not all of these are equally suitable for every age group. Fifteen-year-olds will not show the same enthusiasm for coming out to help as seven-year-olds. The important thing is to find the key that will unlock the particular group. So don't be afraid to check out with a teacher what those particular pupils are and are not interested in. It can be very handy to know in advance how a group are likely to respond to a word like 'Arsenal' . . .

The most useful resource you have is also one that is easy to forget – yourself. Think back to when you were at school. Didn't you love to find out what your teachers were really like? I remember the delight in our class when we found out a teacher's first name or their age. Well, it is still the same. If you can share something of your own life, you will quickly build a rapport with the pupils and be much more than an anonymous visitor. Talk about your home, your work, your hobby – anything that helps to give you a human face. I had a colleague who took an overhead transparency of her cat with her whenever she visited a school. She was always trying to convince people that it looked like the Joker from *Batman*!

There are a number of excellent books with outlines and suggestions for assemblies. Some of them are listed at the end of this book. There is just one problem with them – teachers buy them too. The chances of this happening may be small, but wouldn't it be awful to find at the end of your assembly that a teacher had done the same assembly the day before? If you have a good enough intelligence system, try to find out beforehand what material the school uses.

WHAT ABOUT WORSHIP?

So far we have really been talking about communication. However, the law requires collective *worship* and the fact is that worship means different things to different people. To some it is going through a liturgy of one kind or another; to others it is about giving worth ('worth-ship') to God. Some are satisfied if pupils are given a time for quiet reflection or the opportunity to join in a prayer. Unfortunately, the law is not at all clear in defining what is meant by worship. All this before we get to the knotty theological problem of whether or not true worship can be compulsory!

Two thoughts may be helpful here. The first is to remember that it is the *school* that carries the responsibility for implementing the law. You will need to find out how the school understands worship. I remember what a head teacher said to a schools worker who had just led an assembly: his comment was that although it was very good, it was not worship because it did not include a prayer. Checking this out beforehand would have meant that the head teacher at least was satisfied.

The other point worth considering is that, whatever else collective worship may be, it is meant to be something different to the other things taking place in school. It is *not* another lesson. Issues can be addressed from a different perspective. Pupils can be given the opportunity to think about their personal response. It can provide what may be the one opportunity in a hectic school day for prayer, meditation or contemplation. However, I would want to add two cautions here. First, we need to provide opportunities, not demand actions that are unreal. So we can invite pupils to join us in a prayer rather than assume they will join in. Prayer is not an enforced form of words; it is communion with God and therefore not to be taken lightly. I am sometimes surprised by Christians who in one context are very outspoken about the emptiness of 'formal religion', yet when it comes to school are happy for it to be imposed on everyone. I want pupils to recognise Christian faith as reality, not see it as something that is simply part of the routine of school.

ON THE DAY

Getting to the right place in good time and with everything you need is obviously your first priority. The things we discussed earlier about making contact with a school still apply (chapter three), so introduce yourself at the office unless you have made another arrangement. Having met the teacher who is looking after you, try to see the room in which the assembly will take place. If you have equipment to set up, this will be a necessity. In any case it is well worth it. You will start to get the feel of what you will be involved in.

Schools vary a great deal in how you are brought in to assembly. Some are very formal, others the opposite. Definitely the worst option in my book is when you are marched down the aisle alongside the head teacher, through lines of standing, silent pupils. And the head then introduces you and gets your name wrong.

At last, it is just you and your audience, or rather audiences. Because whether they are eager five-year-olds or cynical adolescents, there is a second audience with them and that is the staff. Sadly, it is all too easy to get through to the pupils yet alienate the teachers and sometimes vice versa. You need to be speaking to both groups. Both will be looking for different things, so there is quite a skill involved in handling this. Pupils will want you to interest and amuse them. If you do a good job, they will come away thinking and open to new ideas. Teachers will want this too, but they will also be looking at your assembly with a professional eye. The acid test for many will be whether you really made contact with the pupils. Some may have preconceived and negative ideas about what someone like you will do, possibly based on past experience. You have to try to win them over if you can. The most important assessment of what you did may well be afterwards in the staff room, and you might never know about it!

The opening is the most crucial part of what you do. If you don't establish contact with the audience quickly, it will be uphill all the way. Unfortunately, this is also the point at which you will be most nervous. So make sure that you know exactly how you are going to begin – script it if you can. Make sure you have a hook that will catch people's attention. Remember that your nervousness will probably make you speak too quickly, so make a conscious effort to slow down. The speed will only sound strange to you.

Humour is a very useful tool but you will need to handle it carefully. It is all too easy for your humour to be a denial of the message you are trying to convey. So don't make jokes at other people's expense. If you want to make someone look foolish, make a joke against yourself. Likewise, there are some subjects that are off limits – race and gender, for example. Don't make jokes about the school or teachers – it will look like a cheap way of getting the pupils on your side, and it won't help the school at all in what they are trying to achieve. In all these cases the problem is not that people won't laugh – many will; but some people will go away remembering that your humour was a bit off and forget what you really wanted to communicate.

Humour must also be good. There is nothing worse than a joke that falls flat. I once took an assembly of 1,500 secondary pupils. We performed a sketch we had used a number of times that involved a couple of jokes. Each one was greeted by total silence. Not even a smirk. We couldn't understand why, so we tried it the next day in another school. This time we got the usual laughs and our confidence was restored. The conclusion we drew was that the pupils in the first school were simply not used to humour in assembly and didn't know how to react. It is difficult to be prepared for that kind of situation. Nevertheless, if we had asked what usually happened, we may have picked up that they were used to a very formal assembly.

Avoiding the pitfalls will be no good, of course, if people cannot hear you. The larger the room or hall, the harder it will be for your voice to carry. You will need to speak loudly and clearly, remembering that the acoustics are different when the room is full of people. The school sound system could be a blessing or a curse, so watch out. Standing at a fixed microphone behind a lectern may feel very frustrating, but if the alternative is not to be heard, the choice is clear.

Try to think ahead about the words you use. The chances are that if there is another way of interpreting the words you say, someone – or more likely everyone – will take the wrong meaning. Most teachers develop a sixth sense which helps them avoid saying the thing that will bring the house down. Unfortunately, you can never be completely ahead of the pupils. I remember noticing a group giggling every time I used the phrase 'getting on with your friends'. It was innocent enough to me and I had never had any problem using the phrase in other schools, but I soon made sure that I said it in a different way if I possibly could.

THREE THORNY ISSUES

Finally, let's look at three traditional, but thorny, components of assembly – singing, the Bible and prayer. Singing is probably the first thing that most older adults think of when they remember school worship. Yet today, the school that gets its adolescents to sing hymns in assembly is very much the exception rather than the rule. The reason is usually practical rather than ideological. There has been a change in our culture and the tradition of community singing has largely been lost. Most adults sing in one of only two situations – when they are alone in the bath or when they are drunk! So in most secondary schools getting pupils to sing in assembly is a lost cause apart from, perhaps, in a carol service. I know that there are exceptions, but this is the general state of affairs. The consequence of this for visitors is that unless we have quite exceptional talent we are on a very sticky wicket if we try to get teenagers singing in assembly. The combined forces of peer pressure and breaking voices are probably too great.

Primary schools are, of course, rather different. It goes without saying that seven-year-olds respond differently to fifteen-year-olds when it comes to singing. Just where the changeover occurs I am not quite sure! However, there is a different issue for us to face here. Whilst there is usually plenty of enthusiasm for singing, we need to be careful in *what* we ask children to sing. It is very tempting to decide on the basis of a good tune, but many very pleasant songs put words into children's mouths that are probably not true for them. Was the school classic 'O Jesus I have promised/ to serve thee to the end' ever a very honest expression of reality for most pupils? I think it is best to avoid songs that are subjective and make children express feelings towards God which may not really be true. It is much better to stick to songs that make more objective statements.

How you use – or perhaps don't use – the Bible is another issue to consider. Waving a telephone-directory-sized black volume around may simply confirm the prejudices of some people. On the other hand, not to use it is to miss a golden opportunity to show something of the Bible's relevance. Whatever you do, make sure you use a translation that is easily understandable and in a format that doesn't look too imposing – a small soft-backed Bible will look a bit more approachable to most people.

Many of the people you are speaking to will have prejudices about the Bible: 'It's not relevant', 'You can't believe it' and 'It's boring' are likely to be three of them. In the minds of most of your audience it probably won't have a great deal of authority. This means that simply quoting the Bible is not likely to be very effective. Equally, reading long chunks is not likely to work very well either unless it is done extremely well. If, on the other hand, you personalise it, talking about why you believe it is important, you begin to establish its credibility with the pupils. In the same way, showing that the Bible contains information and ideas that make sense today can lead people to look at it more seriously. Try using James 4:1–3 and its explanation of the root cause of fighting and quarrels as a way of establishing the relevance of the Bible with pupils.

We have already mentioned the issue of prayer, and what you do in this regard will probably depend upon the normal practice of the school. If you do pray, be prepared to explain what you are going to do. You may want to suggest that pupils echo your prayer silently if they agree with it. In other situations a time of silence may be more appropriate. Whatever you do, try to avoid embarrassing pupils, and make sure that you don't encourage them to say and do things they do not believe.

AND FINALLY
After it is all over, it is tempting to breathe a sigh of relief and enjoy a well-earned cup of coffee. One advantage of staying behind for coffee is that it gives you the chance to get some feedback on what you have done. Feedback is vital if you are going to develop, so be brave! Even better, see if you can get some comments a few days later. You will be a bit less emotionally involved then, and it will be easier to accept criticism. Feedback will enable you to adapt that assembly idea for next time, whether in a different school or in the same school with a different group. However, in asking for comment, you are also making a statement to the school. You are saying that you are concerned about quality and you value their opinion. After all, this is not a bad way to develop a long-term relationship with a school.

SUMMARY

- Before leading an assembly, check:
    the date
    the starting time (and the time you should arrive)
    the actual time that is available to you
    the age range of the pupils
    the number of pupils
    the location (the hall? the dining room?)
    the facilities available
    your subject or theme
    pupils' expectations
    teachers' expectations
    what to avoid
    what you should wear

- When you are deciding what to do:
    aim for one clear idea
    make it relevant to the pupils' age and experience
    choose a method that is suitable for the occasion
    remember – younger pupils may want to come out and
        help; older ones won't
    the law requires an act of worship; think carefully
        about singing, how you use the Bible and prayer

- On the day:
    arrive on time
    think of your audience
    have a well-prepared opening
    make sure you can be heard
    use humour sensitively
    choose your words carefully

- When the assembly is over, try to get helpful feedback
    from the school.

10

IS IT WORTH IT?

I used to laugh at one of those 'only in America' stories about a child who failed kindergarten. Sadly, given the current emphasis on testing everything in sight, I fear that it no longer qualifies as a joke. Someone somewhere has no doubt failed kindergarten for real.

Assessment is a major concern in schools and this, whether it is testing and examinations for pupils, the suggestion of performance testing for teachers or league tables for schools, reflects the trend in society as a whole. The key word is 'measurable', and this area has become a major consumer of teachers' time and energy.

The issue of evaluation faces us in Christian ministry too. It seems obvious that we should ask ourselves hard questions about any kind of ministry in which we are involved. None of us wants to invest time and energy in things that are of little or no value. Life is short, so we must make judgements about the best ways to use the resources God has given us. After all, we are responsible to him for how we use them. So it seems to me that there is no problem with the basic idea that we should evaluate our work.

Things become more difficult when we have to decide *how* to assess the value of our ministry. For some Christians the answer is obvious: we look at how many people have become Christians. This can lead to crass results. An overseas mission organisation advertised the cost of one person coming to Christ through its ministry as evidence of its cost-effectiveness. It implied that you could work out how many people would become Christians as a result of your gift. Another disturbing example was a British church that advertised for an evangelist and offered performance-related pay. Presumably if the poor (probably a good word in this case) evangelist produced no converts, the church produced no pay.

Although the number of conversions seems such an obvious way to evaluate ministry, there are some real problems with it. For one thing, it only takes into account the point at which a person becomes a Christian. Yet for many if not most people, commitment to Christ follows a whole series of events and influences that have often taken place over many years. The impact of much of our work with young people will only be seen later in their lives, and even then the connection is not easily made. I know one person who became a Christian in her early twenties and only then looked back and recognised the influence of a Christian teacher in her secondary school.

A second serious problem with this as the method of assessment is that it tends to see evangelism as a merely human enterprise. It is all up to the evangelist. However, the Bible is clear that God is involved too. As Paul said, 'I planted the seed, Apollos watered it, but God made it grow' (1 Cor 3:6,7). So the number of people becoming Christians is a measure of what *God* has done, not of how effective we have been.

If we are going to evaluate our work effectively and avoid needless frustration, we need to start with a crucial principle, which is simply that *evangelism is a process*. Paul and Apollos were involved in two different activities. First, Paul 'planted the seed'. He made contact with these people who subsequently came to Christ, and shared something of the gospel with them. Apollos then followed on from Paul and 'watered it'. The general response of people to the gospel was not immediate: the seed had to be nurtured. Paul and Apollos avoided a hit-and-run approach and were content to wait for God to make the seed of the gospel grow in his own time.

There is no point in trying to put sowing and watering into a hierarchy because both are vital and often difficult to separate. The whole process of evangelism can involve many things: building a relationship, talking about Christ, working through problems, living out the gospel. Not surprisingly, it will usually involve a series of different people. But in the end the outcome is brought about by God. Given this, let's look at some questions that will help us to evaluate the effectiveness of our work in schools.

Is what we do a part of a long-term strategy?
If most people take some time to come to faith in Christ, one-off events and approaches are going to be of limited value. It is much better to try to develop ongoing links with a school and individual young people so that there is the opportunity to water the seed as well as plant it. Often, of course, we don't have much choice in the matter. Circumstances in a school change; people move on. Nevertheless, this is no basis on which to build a strategy. It is vital to try to develop the long-term possibilities of what we do.

This is a particularly important issue for people who work on an itinerant basis. You can visit a school and leave with a sinking feeling that you have probably wasted your time because there is no one there to follow through what you have done. Or you can leave with the full knowledge that there is someone who will pick up on it and water the seed you have sown.

If you don't have a long-term strategy, all is not lost! Existing work can be a good basis for the future but you will need to do some thinking. A simple starting point is to ask these questions:

Where are we now?
Where do we want to get to?
What resources do we have?

What resources and opportunities will we need?
What should we do next?

Are we developing long-term relationships with young people?

It is not just a matter of maintaining contact with a school over a period of time. Mission involves relationships with people, which means that we have to ask whether our work enables those long-term relationships with individuals to develop. One result may be that spending time with people becomes more important to us in the long run than simply holding lots of meetings or leading as many assemblies as possible. Watering the seed is vital, and this takes time.

How much of our work is with people who have no other contact with Christians?

So much Christian ministry focuses on people with whom the church is already in contact. Unfortunately, this does not include the majority of young people. They are simply not in touch with the church. So we have to face the stark truth that if we are serious about reaching young people for Christ, we will have to go beyond our comfortable boundaries.

This means knowing what we are trying to achieve. Once we are clear about our aims, we will be well placed to decide what to do. For some of us this will mean developing direct contact with a particular group of young people; for others it may be motivating a group of Christians to help their friends to find Christ; and someone else might put their efforts into supporting a teacher or youth worker who already has that contact with people outside the church. The end result of all of these is that people with no Christian contact find out more about Christ.

There is no way that I would want to put down the value of working with Christians and other people on the fringes of Christian activity. After all, seed needs watering. Nevertheless, we have to face the question of whether we really are reaching the people who have not yet been touched by the gospel. The great danger is that our strategies become clever ways of avoiding the risk of going outside our comfort zone.

Are we spreading the vision?
We are all well aware of our limitations, but the task facing us is too important for it to be restricted by what we can achieve ourselves. Perhaps the most important thing we can do is to pass the vision on to other people. We are all severely limited in the amount of energy we have and the number of relationships we can sustain. Little wonder, then, that Jesus told his disciples to ask God 'to send out workers into his harvest field' (Luke 10:2); but this is one of those prayers about which we can do something ourselves!

Time out from direct involvement with schools, to share the vision with other people, is not wasted. Far from it, it may be the most productive thing we do. We need to become enthusiasts about working in schools, and one of the most effective ways of convincing people of its importance is to involve them. Many schools workers I know watch for every opportunity to take other people into schools with them. It is not just so that they can help, it is to help them get a picture of the opportunities and possibilities available.

Is what we are doing faithful to the gospel?
This is one of the most challenging questions of all. It makes us ask about our communication. Do people understand what we are on about, or are we just saying the 'right' things? Does the way that we operate back up what we say, or is there a contradiction? Are we pointing people to Christ, or are we selling people a religion? These are crucial questions, because the easiest thing in the world for any Christian is to lose sight of the fact that we are God's people, called to share the gospel wherever we are.

This takes us back to the question at the start of the chapter – is it worth it? Perhaps it would be better if I let someone else answer it. I was in a meeting recently where a lady asked if she could speak. Simply and quietly she said, 'One cold rainy day when I was twelve, I slipped into the back of a Christian meeting in school. I didn't know anything much at the time, but two years later I knew for sure that God loved me. Almost thirty years later I am evidence of the importance of schools work.'

Which of the people in schools today will be saying something like that thirty years from now?

APPENDIX

SCHOOLS MINISTRY NETWORK

Schools Ministry Network is a voluntary association of Christian organisations and individuals working with schools. In joining the Network, members commit themselves to its objectives, principles and practice. Membership does not imply that any individual has undergone any particular training or is accredited in any way. Members are ultimately responsible to their own employers or organisations.

The objectives of the network are:
1 To promote integrity of Christian ministry in schools and appropriate standards of practice.
2 To co-operate for strategic planning and placement of people and resources.
3 To share resources and ideas, provide credibility, and give opportunities for fellowship and training.
4 To encourage a wider involvement of Christian churches and organisations in ministry in schools.

Principles and practice
1 We recognise schools to be places of Education and seek to work with them in appropriate ways.
2 We believe Christians have a responsibility to make a positive contribution to the whole schools community.
3 We seek to assist pupils to evaluate Christianity as a way of life by, for example:

- helping them to understand the basic Christian beliefs
- sharing the relevance of Christianity to different areas of life
- assisting pupils in forming and/or clarifying personal values
- supporting ongoing Christian work in schools
- giving pupils a positive experience of meeting Christians
- bringing personal and professional support for Christian teachers

4 We recognise the importance of a strategic, long-term approach and ministry in the school community.

5 We seek to work in conjunction with, and mindful of, the school staff, and not in isolation.

6 We seek to co-operate with other Christians in the school community.

7 We seek to identify and make contact with Christians already working in a school before beginning something new.

8 We will show respect for school administration, staff and parents, and never knowingly undermine them.

9 We will seek to teach Christian principles, while not promoting denominations.

10 We are united in purpose yet affirm our diversity in approach and style, within the parameters of the above.

The Network is for anyone doing significant Christian work in schools, not just full-time school workers. Membership is on the basis of recommendation by another member, and acceptance of the SMN principles and practice. Members receive regular mailings, a full address list of other members and the opportunity to attend an annual conference. See page 141 for the contact address.

ADDRESSES & RESOURCES

These are some of the national organisations working in schools. In addition, there are a number of local and regional organisations. For addresses of organisations in your area, contact the Schools Ministry Network.

Association of Christian Teachers, 94a London Road, St Albans, Hertfordshire, WD1 3DD.

Care for Education, 53 Romney Street, London, SW1P 3RS.

Crusaders, 2 Romeland Hill, St Albans, Hertfordshire, AL3 4ET.

Damaris Project, c/o 53 Romney Street, London, SW1P 3RS. The Damaris Project is working to help Christian youth workers in challenging non-Christians with the inadequacy of their own position.

Discovery, Fairgate House, Kings Road, Tyseley, Birmingham, West Midlands, B11 2AA.

Oasis, 87 Blackfriars Road, London, SE1 8HA.

Schools Ministry Network, 207–209 Queensway, Bletchley, Milton Keynes, Buckinghamshire, MK2 2EB; telephone (01908) 856000, fax (01908) 856111.

Schools Outreach, 10 High Street, Bromsgrove, Worcestershire, B61 8HQ.

Scripture Union in Schools (England & Wales), 207–209 Queensway, Bletchley, Milton Keynes, Buckinghamshire, MK2 2EB; telephone (01908) 856000, fax (01908) 856111.

Scripture Union (Scotland), 9 Canal Street, Glasgow, G4 OAB.

Scripture Union (Northern Ireland), 157 Albertbridge Road, Belfast, BT5 4PS.

Scripture Union (Republic of Ireland), 87 Lower Georges Street, Dun Laoghaire, Co. Dublin.

Youth for Christ, Cleobury Place, Cleobury Mortimer, Kidderminster, Worcestershire, DY14 8JG.

Youth with a Mission, 13 Highfield Oval, Ambrose Lane, Harpenden, Hertfordshire, AL5 4BX.

General resources
A Christian Vision for State Education, Trevor Cooling, SPCK.
Curriculum Unmasked, Mark Roques, Monarch: examines the presuppositions of the curriculum.
Faith at the Blackboard, Brian Hill, Eerdmans: looks at the various issues facing Christian teachers.
RE at the Primary Stage, Ralph Gower, Lion.
Schools Now, Charles Martin, Lion: an overview of education in the light of the 1988 Act.
Teaching in a Multi-racial Society, Maurice E J Hobbs, Association of Christian Teachers.
That They May Learn, Brian Hill, Paternoster: towards a Christian view of education. The 1988 London lectures in Contemporary Christianity.
What do you mean – Christian Education?, Fred Hughes, Paternoster.

Resources for worship in schools

A Really Great Assembly, Graham Knox and Chris Chesterton, Scripture Union/Youth For Christ: secondary school assembly outlines.

Assemblies for Primary Schools, Margaret Cooling, RMEP: three books (autumn, spring and summer) of assembly outlines.

Assembly Line, Andrew Smith, CPAS.

Assembly Point, Graham Knox and David Lawrence, Scripture Union/Youth For Christ: assembly outlines for secondary schools.

The Key to a Good Assembly, Claire Derry and Joanna Pitkin, Scripture Union: assembly outlines for infant schools.

52 Ideas for Secondary School Classroom Assemblies, Janet King, Monarch.

Leading Worship in Schools, Janet King, Monarch: a practical guide for visitors to schools.

Line Up for Assembly, Joanna Pitkin, Scripture Union: classroom assemblies for junior schools.

Worship, Worries and Winners, Terence Copley, National Society.

Resources for Christian pupils

David Lawrence, *The Chocolate Teapot*, Scripture Union: being a Christian at school.

The Superglue Sandwich, David Lawrence, Scripture Union: how to talk to your friends about Jesus.

Resources for voluntary Christian groups in schools

Scripture Union in Schools produces a range of practical resources, including: *The 'E' Manual* – equipping and encouraging Christian groups in schools and colleges; and *An Excellent Work* – taking a lead in your Christian group.

Launchpad, Sue Clutterham, Scripture Union: ideas for 11–13s.

Theme Fun, Lesley and Neil Pinchbeck, Scripture Union: activities, puzzles and ideas for 11–13s.

Springboard, Sue Clutterham and Denise Trotter, Scripture Union: lots of practical ideas for 7–11s.

YOYO 1, 2, 3 and *4*, Peter Graystone, Paul Sharpe and Pippa Turner, Scripture Union, lively resources for age 13+.

Resources for use in the classroom

The following publications are some of the titles produced by the Stapleford Project. They are available from Stapleford House Education Centre, Wesley Place, Stapleford, Nottingham, NG9 8DP; telephone (0115) 9396270.

Christianity Topic Books 1, 2 and *3*, Margaret Cooling, RMEP; practical material, arranged thematically, mainly for primary schools.

Exploring Christian Beliefs in School, Trevor Cooling, Association of Christian Teachers: a very useful booklet providing methodology for classroom teaching.

Key Christian Beliefs: A Faith for Living, Chris Wright, Lion: a full-colour textbook for secondary RE.

Teaching RE in Secondary Schools, Janet King and Deborah Helme (eds), Monarch: ideas from the staff room.

Audio visual resources

Scripture Union produce a wide range of audio cassettes and videos suitable for use in schools. For further details, contact Scripture Union Sound and Vision Unit, 207–209 Queensway, Bletchley, Milton Keynes, Buckinghamshire, MK2 2EB; telephone (01908) 856000, fax (01908) 856111.